Student and Parent Friendly Tutorial Guide to 4th and 5th Grade Math

A Supplemental Guide for Students, Parents, Teachers, Substitutes, Tutors and Home Schoolers

Written by

Donna M. Mosch Craft Murdock

Follows the 4th and 5th Grade
Virginia Standards of Learning

Copyright © 2014 by Donna M. Mosch Craft Murdock.

Library of Congress Control Number:		2014902176
ISBN:	Hardcover	978-1-4931-7096-8
	Softcover	978-1-4931-7097-5
	eBook	978-1-4931-7095-1

All rights reserved. No part of this book may be reproduced or transmitted in any form or by any means, electronic or mechanical, including photocopying, recording, or by any information storage and retrieval system, without permission in writing from the copyright owner.

This book was printed in the United States of America.

Rev. date: 04/26/2014

To order additional copies of this book, contact:
Xlibris LLC
1-888-795-4274
www.Xlibris.com
Orders@Xlibris.com
545389

Acknowledgements

My heartfelt thanks for all the encouragement and support from family and many special friends and fellow teachers. I thank all of my students who weren't afraid to ask questions that made me think of the clearest ways to explain and show, step-by-step, the many concepts for their successful understanding. I am indebted to my sister, Anita J. Mosch and David and Tammy Jenner, whose computer expertise made all of the text and graphics possible. Thanks also go to Susie Stuart and her daughter, Meghan, and Annette Roberts, for their editing skills. A very special thanks to my husband, Ernie, for his unending patience.

Author's Biography

Donna M. Mosch Craft Murdock retired in 2008 after teaching for 38 years in grades 4 – 6. As a graduate of Elmira College, her first 17 years were spent teaching in Elmira, NY for the Rochester Diocese. The remaining time was in Williamsburg, VA. During this time she took numerous courses from Shenandoah University and The College of William and Mary. She retired from York County School Division where she taught 5th grade. Her notes that she gave her math students (the basis for this book) have helped her many students excel on their 5th grade math SOL (Standard of Learning) test.

Table of Contents

Students 6
Parents 7
Teachers 8
Substitutes 9
Tutors 10
Home Schoolers 11
IMPORTANT 12
Math Symbols 13

Chapter 1: MULTIPLICATION 14
Multiplication Table 14
(Times Tables) 14
Multiplication 15
Factors 15
Greatest Common Factor (GCF) 16
Multiples 16
Least Common Multiple (LCM) 16
Times Tables 18
    Special Groups 20
    Groups with the same products 20
    Trick for 9's 20
Properties of Multiplication 21
Prime and Composite Numbers 22
    Factor Trees (Prime Factors) 23
Square and Square Roots 25
Multiplying by 10, 100, or 1000 or More 26
Related Sentences 28
Exponents Show Place – Value Relationships 30

Chapter 2: PLACE VALUE 31
Place Value for Whole Numbers to 100 Billion 33
Rounding Whole Numbers (Estimating) 35
Comparing Whole Numbers 37
Ordering Whole Numbers 38
    Least to Greatest 39
Palindromes 40
Key Words for Word Problems 41
Clue Words 42

Chapter 3: ADDITION AND SUBTRACTION 43
Quick Review of Adding and Subtracting Whole Numbers ... 44
Front-End Estimation 45
Working Backwards in Word Problems 46
Too Little or Two Much Information 47

Chapter 4: DECIMALS 48
Decimals 49
Understanding Decimals 51
Rounding Decimals (Estimating) 52
Equivalent Decimals 53
Comparing Decimals 54
Ordering Decimals 55
Adding and Subtracting Decimals 56
Adding and Subtracting Money 57
Multiplying Whole Numbers 58

Exploring Decimal Patterns	61
Multiplying by 10; 100; 1000; etc.	61
Multiplying Decimals by Whole Numbers or a Decimal	62
Chapter 5: DIVISION	**63**
Division	64
Steps of Division	65
Division by Two Digits in the Divisor	70
Dividing by Three Digits in the Divisor	72
Zeros in the Quotient	75
Dividing Whole Numbers into Decimals	77
Dividing Money	78
Dividing Decimals into Decimals	80
Decimal Patterns in Division by 10; 100; 1000; etc.	81
Divisibility	83
Rules of Divisibility	83
Estimating Quotients	85
Interpreting Remainders	87
Order of Operations	89
Chapter 6: FRACTIONS	**90**
Fractions	91
Equivalent Fractions	94
Simplest Form (SF)	97
Least Common Denominator (LCD)	99
Comparing Fractions	100
Comparing Fractions	103
Ordering Fractions	105
Ordering Fraction and Decimal Combinations	108
Adding and Subtracting Fractions	111
Mixed Numbers and Improper Fractions	113
Comparing Mixed Numbers	117
Ordering Mixed Numbers	118
Estimating Fractions and Mixed Numbers to 0, $\frac{1}{2}$, 1	121
Adding and Subtracting Mixed Numbers	123
Multiplying Fractions	129
Short Cut for Multiplying Fractions	130
Multiplying Mixed Numbers	131
Multiplying Mixed Numbers	131
Dividing Fractions	132
Chapter 7: GRAPHS	**133**
Range, Median, Mode, and Mean	134
Reading and Making Graphs	138
Chapter 8: Measurements	**150**
Measurements	151
Linear Measurement – Length	151
Converting Linear Measurements	154
Adding and Multiplying Linear Measurements	156
Metric System	159
Linear Measurements	159
Centimeters, Meters, and Decimals	163
Activities for Linear Measurements	166
U.S. Customary Weights	167

U.S. Customary Measurements of Capacity 169
    Measuring Basics 169
    Mr. Gallon Man 170
    Basic Measurements of Mr. Gallon Man 171
Metric Weight 173
Converting from Grams to Kilograms 175
Metric Capacity 176
Temperature 178
Figuring Temperatures and Changes 181
Time 182
Calculating and Converting Units of Time 183
Elapsed Time 184
Adding and Subtracting Time 187

Chapter 9: GEOMETRY 188
Geometric Models 189
Symbols 190
Shapes 191
    Types of Quadrilaterals 191
Shapes 192
Comparing Shapes 194
Lines 196
Angles 200
Kinds of Angles 203
Geometric Shapes 205
    Polygons 205
Triangles 206
    Triangles by Angles 206
    Triangles by sides 207
    Quadrilaterals 208
    Types of Quadrilaterals 208
Other Polygons 210
Perimeter 212
Formulas for Perimeter of Rectangles and Squares 213
    Rectangle 213
    Square 213
Converting Perimeter 214
Area 216
Area of a Right Triangle 218
Area of Other Triangles 219
Area of Parallelograms 220
Area of Other Polygons 221
Circles and Circumference 222
Parts of a Circle 223
Circumference 224
Area of a Circle 227
Similar and Congruent Figures 228
Congruence and Motion 229
Symmetry 230
Geometric Solids 232
Prisms 233
Pyramids 235
Exploring Surface Area 236

- Surface Area for a Cube 237
- Volume 238
- Volume Formulas 240
- Connecting Metric Volume, Mass, and Capacity 241
- Nautical Measures 242
  - Distance 242
  - Circular Distance 242
  - Depth 242
  - Speed 242
- Light Year 243

Chapter 10: RATIO AND PROBABILITY 244
- Ratios 245
- Patterns in Ratio Tables 246
- Equal Ratios on a Graph (Coordinates) 248
- Probability 250
- Predicting Outcomes 252
- Tree Diagrams for Probabilities 253
- Expressing Probability as Fractions 254

Chapter 11: PRE-ALGEBRA 256
- Integers 257
  - Absolute Values 257
  - Inverse Property of Addition 257
  - Adding Integers 258
  - Subtracting Integers 259
  - Multiplying of Integers 260
  - Division of Integers 261
- Variables 262
- Function Tables 263
- Multi-Function Rule 265
- Understanding and Writing Equations 266
- Substituting Values for Variables 269
- Solving Equations with Like Terms (Variables) 270
- Roman Numerals 274
- Glossary 275

Students

This book was written especially for you so that you could independently learn how to do all of the basic math concepts and skills needed for all future math skills. This will give you a firm foundation to build from so you can be successful in Algebra, Geometry, Calculus, Trigonometry, Chemistry, and Physics, etc. All of these advanced, higher thinking math skills are needed, in some way, in your future careers. In order to learn these, you must first master the basics that you are learning now. Just like constructing a building, the foundation must be made perfectly or the building will fall down.

The key to mastering these skills is *practice, practice, practice, and practice some more*. Think of your favorite athlete or sports team. They know how to play the game, but they practice constantly before each game. They study plays of the last game to see how they can improve. Your favorite singer or group must practice all the time between performances to be as good as they are. **YOU NEED TO DO THE SAME!!**

I have given you the concepts, explanations, and steps for each skill with examples. It is important for you to read aloud everything so that your eyes and ears help your brain absorb, understand, remember, and learn how to do it. You can make up your own practice problems by simply changing the numbers in the examples. These instructional pages can be used to help you figure out your homework in your textbook, workbook, or worksheets.

HAPPY SUCCESS!!

Parents

I know from many years of having parents telling me how frustrated they feel that they can't help their child with their math homework due to the lack of information in the textbook or workbook pages and worksheets which have very little information and vague directions. This book will give you a refresher course on all the basics you learned in elementary grades. You will see in very clear steps how to do the math concepts so you can help or check to see if your child has an understanding of the process.

As I have told the students, read everything aloud (this helps to stir your memory) for better understanding.

Teachers

This book is a quick reference to be used by you in a whole class instruction, small group or one-on-one situation. This is based on the notes I have given my students over my 38 years of teaching 4th, 5th, and 6th grades.

Except for putting multiplication first, the progression of the skills follows the 5th grade Virginia Standards of Learning (SOL's). I have put multiplication first so that your students start right off learning or reviewing the Times Tables since they are the basic units needed for most math concepts.

This book can be used as a text along with supplementary worksheets, workbook pages, or as a base for notes to give to your student for their own notebook reference to aid them in doing their homework assignments. If you have a student who has been absent for any length of time, this can be used to get the student caught up. Another student can use this to help on a one-on-one tutor session. I know that you can think of other ways this book can be useful.

Substitutes

From experience, I know what it is like when you have little or no preparation time before being called to sub in a classroom. This book will give you a quick reference in all of the math concepts and skills you may need. If you are going to be in a classroom for more than one day, then you now have at your fingertips steps, shortcuts, examples, etc., to help you make math meaningful and less stressful for you and your students.

Tutors

For those of you working with students who need extra help in learning new skills, refreshing their memories, or working with those students who are just struggling with the understanding of the processes needed for success. This will provide you with the explanations and steps students will need.

It is important that you read everything aloud with the student. Ask them to rephrase the explanation, steps, and/or the directions. When they do this, you can tell if they truly understand what to do.

Make up new problems like the examples to confirm their grasp of the concepts.

Home Schoolers

This book is an excellent resource for home schooling students who can work independently at their own pace. Used with other resources or alone, precise instructions and examples help in learning or reviewing math concepts.

If there are several home schoolers working together, they can use this book to help and check each other's work, discussing the procedures and steps for working out the problems. They can take turns making up their own problems by simply changing the numbers in the examples for practice. This book can be used with any supplemental practice workbooks.

IMPORTANT

Read everything <u>aloud</u>. This way you are not only seeing it in your mind's eye, you are also hearing it. This helps to reinforce the material for retaining it.

Read it <u>again</u>, and <u>again</u> as many times as you need to aid understanding.

Math Symbols

+	add, plus sign
-	subtract, minus sign
×	multiply, times sign
÷	divide by, ⟌ division set up
=	equal to
≠	not equal to
>	greater than
<	less than
∅ { }	empty set
≥	greater than or equal to
≤	less than or equal to
:	is compared to, ratio
∞	infinity
∠	angle
∟	right angle
⊥	perpendicular
∥	parallel to
√	square root
≈	approximately equal
|n|	absolute value

Chapter 1:

MULTIPLICATION

Multiplication Table
(Times Tables)

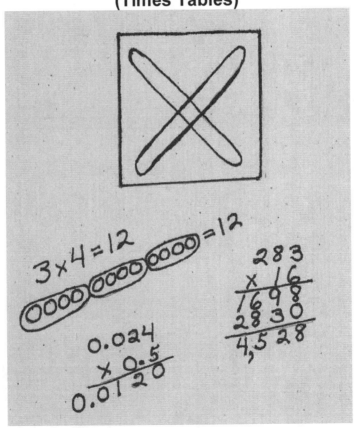

Multiplication

Multiplication is a fast way of adding groups of equal amounts.

Factors are all the numbers you multiply together.

Products are the answers when you multiply factors.

Factors

Factors begin with a letter F as in few, there is a beginning and end.

When asked to give the factors of a certain number, put all of the factors in order beginning with 1 and ending with the number.

Ex: Find the factors of 12.

$12 = \underline{1}, 2, 3, 4, 6, \underline{12}$ begins with 1, ends in 12

Every factor has a partner.

$1 \times 12 = 12, \; 2 \times 6 = 12, \; 3 \times 4 = 12$

Greatest Common Factor (GCF)

To find the GCF, you must find all the factors of each number, and then find the greatest number that is the same in all groups.

Ex: Find the GCF for 12 and 18

```
12 = 1, 2, 3, 4, 6, 12
18 = 1, 2, 3, 6, 9, 18
GCF = 6
```

Multiples

Multiples begins with <u>M</u> for <u>m</u>any numbers, there is <u>NO</u> end.

Multiples are all the <u>products</u> you get when you multiply by a specific number.

<u>All</u> multiples begin with the number given and proceed in order.

Ex: Give the multiples of 5

<u>5</u> = <u>5</u>, 10, 15, 20, 25, 30, 35, 40 . . .

(3 dots mean that the numbers go on and on, there is NO END)

Least Common Multiple (LCM)

To find the LCM, first list the multiples for the two or more numbers given until you find the <u>FIRST</u> (this will be the least – smallest number) number that is the SAME in all groups of multiples.

EX: Find the LCM for 6, 9, and 12

```
6 = 6, 12, 18, 24, 30, 36, 42 . . .
9 = 9, 18, 27, 36, 45 . . .
12 = 12, 24, 36, 48 . . .
LCM = 36
```

When doing fractions the LCM becomes the least common denominator (LCD).

I would tell my 4th graders that they needed to know their times table basic facts frontwards, backwards, inside out and upside down as fast as they could and I would snap by fingers to show them how fast they need to say the answers. They need to be automatic. I would tell them that the majority of math concepts and steps will deal with basic times table facts in some way, including long multiplication, long division, fractions, decimals, figuring measurements, ratios, geometry, and algebra.

As you can see on the times table, each subsequent table is less than the one before it. This is because if you know 3 × 4 = 12, then you automatically know 4 × 3 = 12, so it is not necessary to put it in the next table. This makes it less overwhelming. It seems less to learn.

When you know your multiplication facts, you automatically know your division facts, just turn them around.

Ex:

3 × 4 = 12 so 12 ÷ 3 = 4
4 × 3 = 12 so 12 ÷ 4 = 3

These are called **related sentences** because they ALL have the SAME numbers.

Times Tables

Zero property – any number multiplied by zero equals zero.

Ex:

6 × <u>0</u> = <u>0</u>

Identity property – any number multiplied by one (1) equals the number.

Ex:

<u>6</u> × 1 = <u>6</u>

If <u>ONE</u> or <u>BOTH</u> factors are <u>even</u> numbers, <u>ALL</u> products are <u>even</u> numbers.

Ex:

3 × <u>4</u> = <u>12</u>   <u>4</u> × <u>4</u> = <u>16</u>

If <u>BOTH</u> factors are <u>odd</u> numbers, <u>ALL</u> products are <u>odd</u> numbers.

Ex:

<u>3</u> × <u>3</u> = <u>9</u>

Read everything <u>aloud</u>. This way you are not only seeing it in your mind's eye, you are also hearing it. This helps to reinforce the material for retaining it.

Read it <u>again</u>, and <u>again</u>, as many times as you need to aid understanding.

2's	3's	4's	5's	6's	7's
2 × 2 = 4	3 × 3 = 9	4 × 4 = 16	5 × 5 = 25	6 × 6 = 36	7 × 7 = 49
2 × 3 = 6	3 × 4 = 12	4 × 5 = 20	5 × 6 = 30	6 × 7 = 42	7 × 8 = 56
2 × 4 = 8	3 × 5 = 15	4 × 6 = 24	5 × 7 = 35	6 × 8 = 48	7 × 9 = 63
2 × 5 = 10	3 × 6 = 18	4 × 7 = 28	5 × 8 = 40	6 × 9 = 54	7 × 10 = 70
2 × 6 = 12	3 × 7 = 21	4 × 8 = 32	5 × 9 = 45	6 × 10 = 60	7 × 11 = 77
2 × 7 = 14	3 × 8 = 24	4 × 9 = 36	5 × 10 = 50	6 × 11 = 66	7 × 12 = 84
2 × 8 = 16	3 × 9 = 27	4 × 10 = 40	5 × 11 = 55	6 × 12 = 72	
2 × 9 = 18	3 × 10 = 30	4 × 11 = 44	5 × 12 = 60		
2 × 10 = 20	3 × 11 = 33	4 × 12 = 48			
2 × 11 = 22	3 × 12 = 36				
2 × 12 = 24					

8's	9's	10's	11's	12's
8 × 8 = 64	9 × 9 = 81	10 × 10 = 100	11 × 11 = 121	12 × 12 = 144
8 × 9 = 72	9 × 10 = 90	10 × 11 = 110	11 × 12 = 132	
8 × 10 = 80	9 × 11 = 99	10 × 12 = 120		
8 × 11 = 88	9 × 12 = 108			
8 × 12 = 96				

Special Groups

Squares	Side – by - Side
2 × 2 = 4	2 × 3 = 6
3 × 3 = 9	3 × 4 = 12
4 × 4 = 16	4 × 5 = 20
5 × 5 = 25	5 × 6 = 30
6 × 6 = 36	6 × 7 = 42
7 × 7 = 49	7 × 8 = 56
8 × 8 = 64	8 × 9 = 72
9 × 9 = 81	9 × 10 = 90
10 × 10 = 100	10 × 11 = 110
11 × 11 = 121	11 × 12 = 132
12 × 12 = 144	

Groups with the same products

2 × 6 = 12 3 × 4 = 12	2 × 9 = 18 3 × 6 = 18	2 × 12 = 24 3 × 8 = 24 4 × 6 = 24	3 × 10 = 30 5 × 6 = 30	4 × 10 = 40 5 × 8 = 40
2 × 8 = 16 4 × 4 = 16	2 × 10 = 20 4 × 5 = 20		3 × 12 = 36 4 × 9 = 36 6 × 6 = 36	4 × 12 = 48 6 × 8 = 48

Trick for 9's

Subtract 1 from the other number, this gives you the tens place number, then subtract that number from 9, this gives you the ones place number.

Ex:

There are other tricks for the 9's that uses your fingers, but everyone around you is going to see what you are doing. This trick is done in your head; no one else will know what you are really doing.

Properties of Multiplication

Zero Property – any number multiplied by zero equals zero.

Identity Property – any number multiplied by 1 equals the number.

Commutative Property – the product is the same regardless of the order of factors.
Ex: 3 × 7 = 21   7 × 3 = 21

Associative Property – The product is the same regardless of the grouping of factors.
Ex: (3 × 10) × 7 = 3 × (7 × 10)   * Note – the same numbers are found
          30 × 7 = 3 × 70   on both sides of the equal sign.
            210 = 210

Ex: 30 × 50 = (3 × 10) × (5 × 10) = (3 × 5) × (10 × 10)
                30 × 50 = 15 × 100
                  1500 = 1500

Distributive Property – the distributing property says that multiplication and addition can be linked together by distributing the multiplier over the addends in an equation.

Ex:

$4 \times (2+5) = (4 \times 2) + (4 \times 5)$

  4 × 7 = 8 + 20

   28   =   28

This also means that numbers can be broken down and more than one operation can be used to solve the problem.

Ex:

$4 \times 13 = 4 \times (10+3) = (4 \times 10) + (4 \times 3)$
                40 + 12
                  52

$6 \times 19 = 6 \times (20-1) = (6 \times 20) - (6 \times 1)$
               120 − 6
                114

Prime and Composite Numbers

Reminder – We know that all numbers are either even or odd. <u>All even</u> numbers are multiples of 2. <u>All odd</u> numbers are NOT multiples of 2.

All numbers are either <u>prime</u> or <u>composite</u>.

<u>**Prime numbers**</u> have <u>ONLY</u> <u>TWO</u> factors – the number itself and 1.

Ex: 5 = 1 × 5   No other factors can make 5
         1, 5

<u>**Composite numbers**</u> have MORE than two factors.

Ex: 6 × 1, 6 = 2 × 3   So the factors of 6 are 1, 2, 3, 6 (<u>More</u> than 2 factors)

List of <u>prime</u> numbers –

1, 2, 3, 5, 7, 11, 13, 17, 19, 23, 29, 31 ,37, 41, 43, 47, 53, 59, 61, 67, 71, 73, 79, 83, 89...

List of <u>composite</u> numbers – 4, 6, 8, 10, 12...
(All even numbers except 2 are composite numbers.)

Ex: Odd numbers that are composites:
9, 15, 21, 25, 27, 33, 35, 39, 45, 49, 51, 55, 57, 63, 65, 69, 75, 77, 81, 85, 87, 93, 95, 99...

Factor Trees (Prime Factors)

Factor trees are set up to show a number reduced to its <u>prime factors</u>. The original number goes at the top and is split into 2 factors. If one or more of this factors are not prime then they are split into 2 factors, etc. until only prime factors are left.

Ex: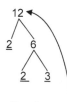

Proof:
(2 × 2) × 3
4 × 3 = 12

(3 × 2) × 2
6 × 2 = 12

Ex: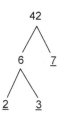

Proof:
(2 × 3) × 7
6 × 7 = 42

Ex: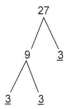

Proof:
(3 × 3) × 3
9 × 3 = 27

Ex: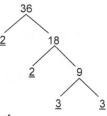

Proof:
(2 × 2) × (3 × 3)
4 × 9 = 36

Ex: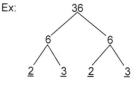

Proof:
(2 × 3) × (2 × 3)
6 × 6 = 36

Ex: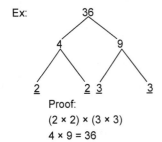

Proof:
(2 × 2) × (3 × 3)
4 × 9 = 36

Square and Square Roots

When number is squared it is raised to the second power.

Ex:

$3^2 = 3 \times 3 = 9$

If you are given a number with the **radical** ($\sqrt{}$) sign around it, this shows that the number is a squared number.

Ex:

So $\sqrt{9}=3$ 3 is the square root of 9.

Table of Square Roots to 50:

$\sqrt{1} = 1$	$\sqrt{361} = 19$	$\sqrt{1369} = 37$
$\sqrt{4} = 2$	$\sqrt{400} = 20$	$\sqrt{1444} = 38$
$\sqrt{9} = 3$	$\sqrt{441} = 21$	$\sqrt{1521} = 39$
$\sqrt{16} = 4$	$\sqrt{484} = 22$	$\sqrt{1600} = 40$
$\sqrt{25} = 5$	$\sqrt{529} = 23$	$\sqrt{1681} = 41$
$\sqrt{36} = 6$	$\sqrt{576} = 24$	$\sqrt{1764} = 42$
$\sqrt{49} = 7$	$\sqrt{625} = 25$	$\sqrt{1849} = 43$
$\sqrt{64} = 8$	$\sqrt{676} = 26$	$\sqrt{1936} = 44$
$\sqrt{81} = 9$	$\sqrt{729} = 27$	$\sqrt{2025} = 45$
$\sqrt{100} = 10$	$\sqrt{784} = 28$	$\sqrt{2116} = 46$
$\sqrt{121} = 11$	$\sqrt{841} = 29$	$\sqrt{2209} = 47$
$\sqrt{144} = 12$	$\sqrt{900} = 30$	$\sqrt{2304} = 48$
$\sqrt{169} = 13$	$\sqrt{961} = 31$	$\sqrt{2401} = 49$
$\sqrt{196} = 14$	$\sqrt{1024} = 32$	$\sqrt{2500} = 50$
$\sqrt{225} = 15$	$\sqrt{1089} = 33$	
$\sqrt{256} = 16$	$\sqrt{1156} = 34$	
$\sqrt{289} = 17$	$\sqrt{1225} = 35$	
$\sqrt{324} = 18$	$\sqrt{1296} = 36$	

Multiplying by 10, 100, or 1000 or More

When you multiply a whole number by 10, simply put one zero to the number because there is one zero in 1<u>0</u>.

Ex: 36 × 1<u>0</u> = 36<u>0</u>

When you multiply by 100, simply put <u>two</u> zeros to the number because there are two zeros in 1<u>00</u>.

Ex: 53 × 1<u>00</u> = 53<u>00</u>

When you multiply by 1000, simply put <u>three</u> zeros to the number because there are three zeros in 1<u>000</u>.

Ex: 283 × 1<u>000</u> = 283,<u>000</u>

If you multiply tens, hundreds, or thousands together, simply count up the zeros and then multiply the remaining whole numbers.

Ex: 3<u>00</u> × 4<u>0</u> = 12,<u>000</u>   (3 zeros on each side of equal sign)

Ex: 2,7<u>00</u> × 5,<u>000</u> = 13,5<u>00,000</u>   (5 zeros on each side of equal sign)
        5 zeros   5 zeros

To find a missing factor, you must divide the product by the given factor. Cross out matching zeros on both sides of the equal sign.

Ex: 80 × ___ = 1,600
     8̶0̶ × __0̶ = 1,60̶0̶   (one zero is left)
     8 × _20_ = 160   (16 ÷ 8 = 2)

Ex: ___ × 600 = 300,000
     _00̶_ × 6̶0̶0̶ = 30̶0̶,0̶0̶0̶   (2 zeros left)
     _500_ × 6 = 3,000

(You can only cross out two zeros on each side because 6 won't go into 3 but it will go into 30 which leave two zeros, and 30 ÷ 6 = 5, so the missing factor is 500.)

When factors are grouped, usually do what's in the parentheses first.

Ex: 14 (5 × 20)   Ex: 100 × (4 × 60)   (100 × 60) × 4
     14 × 100   100 × 240   or   6000 × 4
     1,400   24,000   24,000

Sometimes you can change the grouping to make it easier to figure out the answer.

Ex: (34 × 25) × 4   (Look for factors that can make 10, 100, or 1000, etc.)
    34 × (25 × 4)
    34 × 100
    3400

Ex: 2 × (63 × 5)
    (2 × 5) × 63
    10 × 63
    630

Related Sentences

In <u>addition</u>, related sentences have the same three numbers, both addends are on one side of the equal sign and the sum is on the other side of the equal sign. The addends are the smaller (**s**) numbers and the sum is the largest (**L**) numbers.

Ex: s + s = L   s + s = L   L = s + s
     3 + 4 = 7   4 + 3 = 7   7 = 3 + 4

In <u>Subtraction</u>, the largest (**L**) number <u>always</u> comes FIRST, then the minus sign.

Ex: L – s = s   L – s = s
     7 – 3 = 4   7 – 4 = 3

The complete set of related sentences for the above would be:

 3 + 4 = 7   All four sentences have the **SAME** numbers.
 4 + 3 = 7
 7 – 4 = 3
 7 – 3 = 4

If you are asked to find a missing part, ask yourself the following questions.

Ex: 9 + x = 12   Are you looking for a small number or the largest number?
     s + s = L   Put s's and L

Since you are looking for a small number, you must subtract.

 12 – 9 = 3
 so 9 + 3 = 12
      x = 3

Ex: x – 8 = 9   Are you looking for a small number or the largest number?
     L – s = s

Since you are looking for the largest number, you must add.

 8 + 9 = 17
 x = 17

Replace the x for 17, is it now correct?

 17 – 8 = 9   Yes!

These same steps work for multiplying and dividing related sentences.

× is the same rule as +; ÷ is same as − rule.

Ex: s × s = L   s × s = L
     4 × 5 = 20   5 × 4 = 20

Ex: L ÷ s = s   L ÷ s = s
     20 ÷ 4 = 5   20 ÷ 5 = 4

Complete set of related sentences for above.

    4 × 5 = 20   All four sentences have the **SAME** numbers.
    5 × 4 = 20
    20 ÷ 5 = 4
    20 ÷ 4 = 5

Find a missing number:

Ex: s × s = L
     6 × x = 18

You are looking for a small number, so you must divide.

    18 ÷ 6 = 3

Substitute the x with 3.

    6 × 3 = 18

Does this make it correct? Yes!

Ex: L ÷ s = s
     x ÷ 7 = 4

You are looking for the largest number, so you must multiply.

    7 × 4 = 28

Substitute x with 28

    28 ÷ 7 = 4

Does this make it correct? Yes!

Exponents Show Place – Value Relationships

Base 10
1$\underline{00}$ = 1$\underline{0}$ × 1$\underline{0}$ = 10^2 (This is read as 10 to the second power)
^{2} is the exponent, it shows that ten times ten equals 100. The exponent tells how many zeros are at the end of the number.

1,$\underline{000}$ = 1$\underline{0}$ × 1$\underline{0}$ × 1$\underline{0}$ = 10^3 (Ten to the third power)
10,$\underline{000}$ = 1$\underline{0}$ × 1$\underline{0}$ × 1$\underline{0}$ × 1$\underline{0}$ = 10^4 (Ten to the fourth power)
1$\underline{00}$,$\underline{000}$= 1$\underline{0}$ × 1$\underline{0}$ × 1$\underline{0}$ × 1$\underline{0}$ × 1$\underline{0}$ = 10^5 (Ten to the fifth power)
1,$\underline{000}$,$\underline{000}$ = 1$\underline{0}$ × 1$\underline{0}$ × 1$\underline{0}$ × 1$\underline{0}$ × 1$\underline{0}$ × 1$\underline{0}$ = 10^6 (Ten to the sixth power)

1,000,000,000 = 10^9 (9 is the exponent because there are 9 zeros)

How many 100's are in 10,000?
You need to divide 10,000 by 100.

*Shortcut – cross out matching zeros on both numbers.
    10,0̶0̶0̶ ÷ 1̶0̶0̶

What is left?   100
Answer is 100, so there are 100 hundreds in 10,000.

How many 1,000's are in 1 million?
Change 1 million to 1,000,000.
Cross out matching zeros.
    1,000,0̶0̶0̶ ÷ 1,0̶0̶0̶
What is left?   1,000
Answer is 1,000, so there are 1,000 thousands in 1 million.

If your base is 5, then the exponent tells how many times you will multiply by 5.

Ex: 5^3 = 5 × 5 × 5 = 125
      5^6 = 5 × 5 × 5 × 5 × 5 × 5 = 15,625

If your base is 3, then the exponent tells how many times you will multiply by 3.

Ex: 3^5 = 3 × 3 × 3 × 3 × 3 = 243
            9 × 3
              27 × 3
                81 × 3
                  243

Chapter 2:

PLACE VALUE

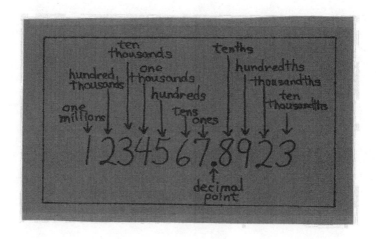

Counting Numbers or Natural Numbers begin with 1 and continue into infinity. 1, 2, 3, 4, 5, 6, 7, 8, 9, 10…

Whole Numbers begin with 0 and go into infinity. 0, 1, 2, 3, 4, 5, 6, 7, 8, 9, 10…

Rational Numbers include any number than can be written in the form of a fraction as long as the denominator is not equal to 0.

All counting and whole numbers can be written as fractions with a denominator equal to 1. So, all counting and whole numbers are also rational numbers.

All counting numbers and whole numbers are <u>integers</u>.

Integers include 0, all of the counting numbers (positive whole numbers) and the whole numbers less than 0 (negative numbers).

Digits – any single numeral 0 through 9.

Numeral – any symbol which stands for a number: 0, 1, 2, 3… are Arabic numerals and the following are Roman numerals: I, II, III, IV, V….

Place Value for Whole Numbers to 100 Billion

Billions				Millions				Thousands				Ones		
Hundred billions	Ten billions	One billions		Hundred millions	Ten millions	One millions		Hundred thousands	Ten thousands	One thousands		Hundreds	Tens	Ones
3	2	1	,	9	8	7	,	6	5	4	,	3	2	1

Each group heading is called a <u>period</u>.

Commas separate the periods.

Every digit in a number has its own position and value.

Ex: 654,321   (from above)
Position of 5 is in the ten thousands place

Value of the 5 — 654,321
                      ↓
                   50,000   (bring 5 down, all digits on right go to zero)

Ex: 21,987,654,321   (from above)
Position of 9 is in the hundred millions place.

Value of the 9 — 21,987,654,321
                          ↓
                   900,000,000   (bring 9 down, all digits on right go to zero)

Standard Form - When the digits are right next to each other, the number is in standard form.

Ex: 834,657

Written Form - of the above number is eight hundred thirty-four thousand, six hundred fifty-seven

(A comma MUST be put after the name of the period name – thousand)

Expanded Form
Each digit is written as its value form with a plus sign in between each value. When you add up all the values, you get the standard form.

Ex: 834,657
       800,000 + 30,000 + 4,000 + 600 + 50+ 7

       Add together -   800,000
                                    30,000
                                      4,000
                                        600
                                          50
                               +   7
                             834,657 Standard Form

Whole numbers begin with 0 and proceed in sequence.

Ex: 0, 1, 2, 3, 4, 5...

* Remember 3 dots indicate that there is NO end.

Natural numbers are counting number, beginning with 1 and continue in order.

Ex: 1, 2, 3, 4, 5...

Multiplication problems use a times sign (×), a number before parenthesis or a dot (•).

Ex: 3 × 4 = 12
       3(4) = 12
       3 • 4 = 12

When a number is before a letter, which represents an unknown, you would multiply the number times the value of the unknown.

Ex: $3n$ means 3 times n, if $n = 6$, then 3 × 6 = 18

Rounding Whole Numbers (Estimating)

Using a number line makes rounding easy to understand.

(5 is <u>always</u> in the middle)

43 = 40 because 43 is between 40 and 50, since 43 is less than 45 (the halfway mark), it is <u>closer</u> to 40.

Greater numbers work the same way.

Ex:

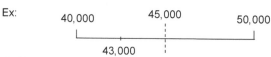

43,000 = 40,000
45,000 is the middle, 43,000 is less so it's closer to 40,000.

Rounding to a specific place:

Ex: 761<u>6</u>59

    Round the underlined digit to the nearest 1,000
    1 is in the one thousands place. Look at the number on the right of the 1 which is **6**.
    This will determine if the 1 stays 1 or goes to 2. Since the 6 is greater than 5, the 1
    goes up to 2.

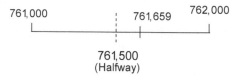

                              761,500
                              (Halfway)

761,659 is greater than halfway so, it is closer to 762,000.
(Everything on the right of the 2 goes to zeros.)

Ex: Round to the nearest million
          269<u>9</u>99,999 = 270,000,000

          The underlined digit is in the millions place, the **9** on the right means the underlined 9
          must go up by 1, since 9 can't go to 10, the 69 must go to 70.

Ex: Round to the nearest ten million
          5,4<u>8</u>3,642,013 = 5,480,000,000

          The 8 stays because there is a **3** on the right, which is LESS than 5.
          Everything on the right goes to zero.

<u>ALWAYS</u> keep everything on the left.

I would tell my students to think about money. If they had $248.75 and were told to round it the nearest $10; the 4 would go to five because of the 8 on the right, the 8, 7 and 5 would go to zeros, but they must keep the two making the answer $250. If they threw the 2 away they would be getting only $50 instead of $250. This impressed upon them to ALWAYS KEEP THE NUMBERS ON THE LEFT.

Points to remember:

- When the digit on the right of the place to round is LESS than 5, the rounded place digit <u>STAYS</u>.
- When the digit on the right of the place to round is 5 or greater, the rounded place digit goes up by one.

Ex: Round to the nearest billion place
79,864,306,462 = 80,000,000,000
8 is greater than 5 so the 9 <u>goes up</u>

Ex: Round to the nearest hundred billion
634,583,124 = 600,000,000,000
3 is less than 5 so, 6 <u>stays</u>

Comparing Whole Numbers

< less than   s < L
> greater than   L > s
= equal to   point of arrow is ALWAYS next to smaller number

Ex:
      s   L
    32 < 74

When two numbers have the same amount of different digits, simply compare the digit at the far left of each number.

Ex: 3̲46 < 6̲82   Since 3 is less than 6, a less sign is put between them.

Ex: 2̲,684 > 1̲,864   Since 2 is greater than 1, a greater sign is used.

When the two numbers have the same number of digits with the same two or three digits on the far left, find the first digit from the left that is different and compare those digits.

Ex: 32,4̲56 < 32,8̲64   Since 32 begins each number; you must look at the 4 and 8.
       4 is less than 8.

When the two numbers being compared have different amount of digits, simply count the number of digits, put how many digits there are above each number and compare those amounts.

             5   4
Ex: 15,689 > 2,694   5 digits is greater than 4 digits.

Of course, if the two numbers are the same, they are equal.

When comparing very large numbers, first look at the number of commas. If they have different amount of commas, the number with the fewer commas is automatically less.

Ex: 1,123,684 > 123,684
       2 commas   1 comma

One comma is less than 2 commas. You don't need to pay any attention to any of the digits.

Ordering Whole Numbers

1. When you put whole numbers in order from least to greatest, FIRST, look at the set of numbers to see if they have <u>different</u> amounts of digits. If they are different, simply order by number of digits.

              3   2   4   5

Ex: 643   49   5,682 12,683   (different amounts of digits)

Answer: 49   643 5,682   12,683
            ordered from least to greatest

2. If the set of numbers have the <u>same</u> amounts of digits, simply look at the digits on the far left to put into order from least to greatest.

Ex: <u>8</u>362 <u>1</u>234 <u>7</u>632 <u>2</u>468

Answer: <u>1</u>234 <u>2</u>468 <u>7</u>632 <u>8</u>362

3. When you are doing greater numbers that have <u>different</u> amounts of digits, FIRST look at commas. If they have all different amounts of commas, simply compare the number of commas.

          2 commas   3 commas   1 comma

Ex: 38,032,964 3,806,942,154 9,486

       Answer: 9,486   38,032,964   3,806,942,154

Sometimes the numbers may have some digits and commas that are the same.

```
                    L              G
Ex:     823,469   18,632   842,715   23,199,471
```

Least to Greatest

Look at commas first – one has 2 commas, others only one so, 23,199,471 is automatically the greatest.

Next, look at the digits on the left parts of the commas of the remaining numbers. 18 is the smallest so, this is the least number.

Now you have two numbers left that have one comma each and the same amount of digits on the left side of the commas so, find the first digit that is smaller.

2 is less than 4 (see underlined digits above). Put in order least to greatest.

Answer: 18,632   823,469   842,715   23,199,471

* Be careful to pay close attention to the directions. If you are asked to put in order from greatest to least, be sure to put the largest number first going to the smallest.

Palindromes

Palindromes are words or numbers that are the same forward or backward.

Ex:

mom   33
dad   262
noon   4554
            636,636

You can make your own palindromes using addition.

Ex:

Choose a number	324
Reverse the number	+423
Add them together	747

You have made a palindrome.

You may have to keep reversing and adding to get a palindrome.

Ex:

```
   59
 + 95   reverse
  ----
  154
 +451   reverse
  ----
  605
 +506   reverse
  ----
 1111   palindrome
```

Key Words for Word Problems

Word problems can be a little confusing when it comes to deciding what operation to use to figure out the answer. It is very helpful to recognize certain word clues that tell you what operation to use.

For <u>addition</u> and <u>multiplication</u> the questions will have "how many", "in all", "what is the total", "altogether", "how much".

In <u>subtraction</u> the questions will have, "how much more", "how many more", "how many were NOT", "how much taller, longer, etc...", "what is the difference", "how much was left", "how much change (money)".

In <u>division</u> the questions will have, "how much will each", "how much will be left over (remainder)", "what is the greatest amount for each", "how many boxes, shelves, etc...", "how many would be needed".

In trying to figure out word problems, put yourself in the problem. Pretend that you are actually doing what the problem is saying. This will help greatly in deciding what operation to use and being able to answer the question in the problem.

Ask yourself certain questions, and writing down the answers.

1. What do I know? What information does the problem give me?

2. What does the question ask?

3. What are the key words? Underline them.

4. How am I going to use the numbers to answer the question?

5. After working it out, does the answer make sense?

If helpful, draw a picture, make a timeline, chart, whatever may help you to understand what is happening in the problem.

Clue Words

Addition

add
sum
total
in all
both
together
increased by
all together
combined

Subtraction

subtract
difference
take away
less than
more than
more
fewer
remaining
have or are left
change (as in money)

Multiplication

times
product of
multiplied by
by (dimensions)
twice as many
twice more than

Division

quotient of
divided by
half (or a fraction)
split
separated
cut up
parts
shared equally
each

Chapter 3:

ADDITION AND SUBTRACTION

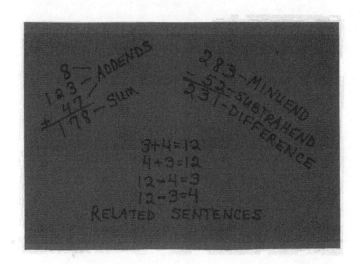

Quick Review of Adding and Subtracting Whole Numbers

Since this is mastered in 2nd and 3rd grade, here are some reminders.

In <u>addition</u>, numbers that are added are <u>addends</u>, the answer is the <u>sum</u>.

All numbers must be lined up correctly by the ones column, tens column, hundreds column, etc. for both adding and subtracting.

Ex:
```
       1 1
       468  ⟍
     2,143  ─→ Addends
   +    75  ⟋
     2,686    Sum
      (10,10)
   Carry the one to the next column
```
to check simply add backwards

```
    2,686    Check
  ▲  468
     2,143
   +   75
```

In <u>subtraction</u>, the largest number ALWAYS goes on top of the problem. This number is called the **minuend**. The number being subtracted is the **subtrahend**. The answer is the **difference**.

If parts of the minuend are too small to subtract from, you must regroup by taking 10, 100, etc. from the left and add it to the digit at the top so it is large enough to subtract.

Short cut:

```
          6 15 10
Ex:      7,608
       -   913
         6,695
```
Regroup at the top so you can subtract.

Long way to show what you are really doing:

```
       500  100
   7000 + 600 + 0 + 8
  -        900 + 10 + 3
                90 + 5
```
You can't subtract 10 from 0 so you borrow 100 from 600 to put in tens place. Now you can subtract 10 from 100.

```
     6000  1500  100
   7000 + 600 + 0 + 8
  -        900 + 10 + 3
   6000 + 600 + 90 + 5
```
1000 is taken from 7000 and given to 500 to make 1500 so you can subtract 900.

Now add up the answer.
```
     6000
      600
       90
    +   5
    6,695
```

To check subtraction, <u>add</u> the subtrahend and difference to get the minuend.

Ex:
```
     7608 ⟵
   -  913   ⟍
     6695   ⟋
     7608 ⟋    Check
```

Front-End Estimation

When you do front-end estimation you first use the last numbers on the left as they are and then use the numbers on the right of them to estimate.

Ex:

x	Then adjust
6283	6283 + 3384 + 2976
3384	200 300 900
+ 2978	
11,000	about 1400
	11,000 + 1400 = 12,400

Ex:

x	Then adjust
586	586 + 131 + 328
131	80 30 20
+328	
900	about 130
	900 + 130 = 1030

Ex:

x	Then adjust
$77.62	$77.62 − $42.25
− $42.25	$7.00 $2.00
$30.00	
	about $5
	$30.00 − $5.00 = $25.00

Working Backwards in Word Problems

Sometimes you have to work backwards to answer the question to a word problem.

Ex:

Danny had soccer practice from 4:30 PM to 6:00 PM. It took 15 minutes to get to practice. He had 30 minutes to do his math homework and 30 minutes to change clothes and have a snack. What time did he get home from school?

Work backwards from 4:30 PM.

$3:15 \quad 3:45 \quad 4:15 \quad 4:30$
$\quad\ \ 30min \ \ \ 30min \ \ \ 15min$

He got home at 3:15 PM.

Ex:

On Saturday, Tammy's donut shop was very busy. After the first hour, she sold half of her donuts. During the second hour she sold 75 more. During the rest of the day, half of the remaining donuts were sold. At closing time she only had 30 left. How many did she start with?

Half of total → $x+75$ $\qquad$ $15 - 30$ left
$\qquad\qquad\qquad\qquad\qquad\qquad\quad 2x$

$$75+15+30=120 \times 2=240$$

How many were sold the first hour? __120__ (120 is half of 240)

Too Little or Two Much Information

Word problems with <u>too little</u> information cannot be solved.

Ex:

Joe had to be at his soccer game 15 minutes before it started. The game ended at 6:30. What time did he get to the soccer field?

You cannot find the answer because you don't know what time the game started, or how long it lasted.

Some word problems have <u>too much</u> information and you have to figure out what information is not needed to answer the question.

Ex:

Michael lives 3 miles from school, 6 miles from the library, and $2\frac{1}{2}$ miles farther than Lee's house. How far is Lee's house from school?

Too much information, the question is asking about Lee's house from school compared to Michael's house. So information about the library is not needed to answer the question.

Lee lives $\frac{1}{2}$ mile from school.

Chapter 4:

DECIMALS

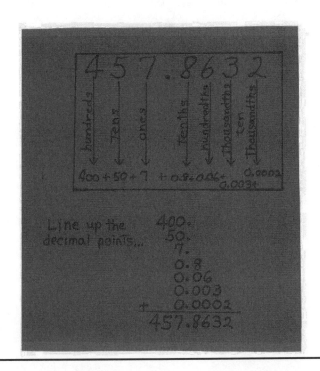

Decimals

Decimals show parts of a whole, an amount less than one whole. Think of money, $1.00 is one whole dollar; $0.63 is less than one dollar.

To show the difference between the whole number and the decimal part, a decimal point is used. All numbers on the left side of the decimal point are whole numbers. All numbers on the right side of the decimal point are the decimal numbers.

Place Value for whole numbers and decimals:

Ten thousands	One Thousands		Hundreds	Tens	Ones	and	Ten<u>ths</u>	Hundred<u>ths</u>	Thousand<u>ths</u>
1	2	,	3	4	5	.	6	7	8

Notice that the names of the places on the right of the decimal point each have <u>ths</u> on the end. When you read a decimal number you MUST say the ending sound distinctly.

Also notice that above the decimal point is the word <u>AND</u>. This must be said when reading it.

The number is read as: twelve thousand, three hundred forty-five <u>AND</u> six hundred seventy-eight thousand<u>ths</u>.

The 8 is in the thousand<u>ths</u> place.

Other examples of how to read decimals:

1. 345.6 – three hundred forty-five AND six ten<u>ths</u>
2. 4.10 – four AND ten hundred<u>ths</u>
3. 52.24 – fifty-two AND twenty-four hundred<u>ths</u>
4. 9.600 – nine AND six hundred thousand<u>ths</u>
5. 0.08 – eight hundred<u>ths</u>
   (No whole number, 8 is in the hundred<u>ths</u> place)

In no. 1 above, the 6 is in the tenths place.
In no. 2 above, the 0 is in the hundredths place.
In no. 3 above, the 4 is in the hundredths place.
In no. 4 above, the last 0 is in the thousandths place.
In no. 5 above, the 8 is in the hundredths place.

If there is NO whole number, you just read the decimal side, as in no. 5.
If there is NO whole number you MUST put <u>one</u> <u>zero</u> on the left side of the decimal point to show that there is NO whole number.

Understanding Decimals

An easy way to understand decimals is to look at money.

100 pennies (cents) = 1 whole dollar
Using a dollar sign and a decimal point, we write one dollar as $1.00.

Less than a whole dollar such as seventy – five cents is written as $0.75 means 75 pennies out of 100 pennies.
> If you take away the dollar sign, you would read this as seventy-five hundredths because the five is in the hundredths place.

Three cents is written as $0.03. This means three pennies out of 100 pennies.
> If you take the dollar sign away, you would read this as three hundredths because the three is in the hundredths place.

Centa means 100 as in a century equals 100 years.

Deca means 10 as in a decade is 10 years.

Ten cents is written as $0.10. Since ten cents is a dime and ten dimes make a dollar, 0.1 is one tenth (one tenth of a dollar).

You can always add a dollar sign to double check to see if your decimal has been written correctly and makes sense.

Rounding Decimals (Estimating)

When you round decimals, you round the <u>same</u> way you round whole numbers – you round to the place indicated or underlined place.

Ex: Round to the nearest <u>whole number</u>.

   13(6) = 14.0 or 14   3 is in the whole number place, 6 is the right so the 3 goes to 4

* <u>Note</u> – 4 and 4.0 equal the same amount. Every whole number has a decimal point on the right even if you don't see it, it really is there.

Ex: Round to the nearest <u>tenths place</u>.

   2.4(6) = 2.50 or 2.5   The 6 makes the 4 go to 5.

Ex: 0.9(7) = 1.00 or 1   The 7 makes 9 go to 10.

Ex: 75.3(2) = 75.0 or 75.3   The 2 makes the 3 stay.

* <u>Note</u> – if there is a 0 on the far right of the decimal side, it can be left out.

Round to the nearest hundredths place:

Ex: 0.82(6) = 8.830 or 0.83

   5.12(3) = 5.120 or 5.12

   4.99(9) = 5.000 or 5

   (Underlined 9 must go up by 1, so 99 + 1 = 100, 4.99 + 1 = 5.00 or 5)

Round to the nearest whole number:

Ex: 2.(4)6 = 2.00 or 2

   0.(8)42 = 1.000 or 1

   29.(2)3 = 29.00 or 29

   0.(4) = 0

Equivalent Decimals

When you have two decimals that have the same numbers except one has an extra zero on the decimal side at the far right, you can add a "magic zero" to the one that doesn't have the zero to make them equivalent.

Ex:
    3.4 = 3.40
    3.4^0 = 3.40

> A small "magic zero" is added to the 4 on the left and you can see they are equal

Ex:
    52.060 = 52.06
    52.060 = 52.06^0

Ex:
    0.900 = 0.9
    0.900 = 0.9^{00}

Find the equivalent decimal in each group:

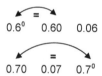

0.6^0 0.60   0.06

0.70   0.07 0.7^0

Using a "magic zero" makes it easy to see which ones are equivalent.

* Note – At this time the "magic zero" is not meant to be used as an exponent. It is just to help in the understanding of equivalency.

Comparing Decimals

When you are comparing decimals, FIRST, look at the whole number side. If you have different whole numbers, simply compare the whole numbers. You don't even have to look at the decimal side.

Ex:

    2<u>3</u>.6 > <u>3</u>.48

    2<u>84</u>.65 < <u>842</u>.7

If the whole numbers are the same, look at the decimal side. Even up the digits if they are different amounts by adding "magic zeros".

Ex:

    2.6<u>1</u> < 2.6<u>8</u>

    0.<u>92</u>^{0} > 0.<u>743</u>

* <u>Note</u> – by adding a "magic zero" so there are 3 digits on the decimals sides, it's easy to see that 920 is greater than 743.

Ex:

    0.461 > 0.4^{00}

    3.6^0 < 3.62

    68.05 < 68.5^0

    11.6^{00} = 11.600

Ordering Decimals

If all the numbers have different whole numbers, simply order by the whole numbers. You don't even have to look at the decimal sides.

Be careful to follow the directions for ordering least to greatest or greatest to least.   L G   G L

Ex: L to G

$\underline{5}$.9 $\underline{2}$.67 $\underline{9}$.2 $\underline{3}$.91

Answer: 2.97   3.91   5.9   9.2

If the whole numbers are the same, look only at the decimal sides. FIRST, even up the number of digits using "magic zeros" if necessary.

Ex: L to G

0.$\underline{2}$3   0.$\underline{1}$6   0.$\underline{1}$1   0.$\underline{0}$3

Answer: 0.03   0.11   0.16   0.23

Ex: L to G

4.8$\underline{3}$ 4.0$\underline{3}$ 4.8^0 4.$\underline{4}$3   * Note "magic zero" added to 8

Answer: 4.03   4.43   4.8   4.83

* Note – the final answer MUST be written using original numbers.

Ex: L to G

23.008   23.1^{00} 23.52^0 23.^{000}

Answer: 23   23.008   23.1   23.52

Using "magic zeros" evens up all the decimal sides so there are three decimal numbers for each.

Adding and Subtracting Decimals

When you add or subtract decimal numbers, the decimal points MUST be lined up directly under each other in order to add or subtract correctly. If necessary add "magic zeros".

EX:
    $6.42 + 21.034 + 0.508$

$$\begin{array}{r} \overset{1}{6.42}{}^{0} \\ 21.034 \\ +\ 0.508 \\ \hline 27.962 \end{array}$$

*Note – decimal points are directly under each other AND a "magic zero" is after the 2

EX:
    $23.4 - 9.58$

$$\begin{array}{r} {}^{1\ 12\ 13}\!\!\!\cancel{23.4}{}^{10} \\ -\ \ \ 9.58 \\ \hline 13.82 \end{array}$$

*Note – you can NOT subtract 8 from nothing so a "magic zero" is put next to the 4, now you can do normal subtraction.

* Note – Before you start to add or subtract, put the decimal point in the proper place in the answer, then add or subtract. This guarantees the decimal point from being left out. Even if you have all the correct numbers for your answer, it will be wrong if the decimal point is missing.

Adding and Subtracting Money

When you have money problems, you MUST FIRST put the dollar sign and decimal point in the answer place before you add or subtract to insure that it won't be left out.

Ex:

$8.14 + $52.03 + $0.87

```
  $52.03
    8.14
 +  0.87
  $   .          Then add
```

*Note – put the largest amount on top

Ex:

$22.94 – $6.33

```
  $22.94
 -  6.33
  $   .          Then subtract
```

Multiplying Whole Numbers

Parts of a multiplication problem:

      top number – multiplicand
  x   multiplier
      product (answer)

When you multiply by one digit, you'll have one row of numbers after you multiply. This is your product (answer).

Ex:

$$\begin{array}{r} \overset{1\ 2}{4\ 3\ 7} \\ \times\ \ 4 \\ \hline 1748 \end{array}$$ (product)

Ones place at the top is ALWAYS multiplied <u>first</u>
4 × 7 = 28, put 8 only down and carry the 2
Next, 4 × 3 = 12, add 2 = 14. Put only the 4 down and carry the 1
Finally, 4 × 4 = 16, add 1 = 17

When you multiply by two digits, you will have two rows that must be added to get the final product.

Ex:

$$\begin{array}{r} 437 \\ \times\ 34 \\ \hline 1748 \\ +1311\underline{0} \\ \hline 14{,}858 \end{array}$$ (product)

On the second row, a zero <u>MUST</u> be put under the 8 so that you can multiply everything at the top by 3
The first number on the second row must go under three

When you multiply by three digits, you will have three rows to add. The third row <u>MUST</u> have two zeros.

Ex:

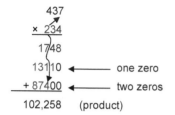

```
      437
   x  234
     1748
    13110    ←——— one zero
   + 87400   ←——— two zeros
   102,258   (product)
```

> Two zeros must go in row three because the first number when you multiply 2 × 7 = 14, the 4 <u>MUST</u> go under the 2 in the multiplier

To make sure of the correct placement of all the digits, you may need to practice on graph paper.

Ex:

			3	7	8	2
				×	5	6
		2	2	6	9	2
+1	8	9	1	0	0	
2	1	1,	7	9	2	

One "magic zero"

59

Multiplication problems can use the times sign × or a • to show that the numbers need to be multiplied.

Ex:
    3 × 4 = 12   3 • 4 = 12

When a number is right in front of a letter, it means that whatever the value of the letter is, it's to be multiplied by the number.

Ex:
    $3x$ means 3 times the value of x

    if $x = 6$ then $3x$ means $3 \times 6 = 18$

If you have a number before a set of parenthesis, you multiply the value of what is inside the parenthesis by that number.

Ex:
    4(3 + 5)   or   (4 × 3) + (4 × 5)
    4 × 8 = 32   12   +   20
                                     32

Exploring Decimal Patterns
Multiplying by 10; 100; 1000; etc...

1. To multiply decimals by 10, simply move the decimal point <u>one</u> place to the <u>RIGHT</u> because there is only <u>one</u> zero in 1<u>0</u>.

    Ex:

    2.24 × 10

    2.24 × 10 = 22.4

    * <u>Note</u> – this is a shortcut. This is what you are really doing:

    2.24
    × 10
    22.40

2. To multiply by 100, simply move the decimal point <u>two</u> places to the <u>RIGHT</u> because there are <u>two</u> zeros in 1<u>00</u>.

    Ex:

    0.248 × 100 = 24.8

    * <u>Note</u> – zero on left goes away.

3. To multiply decimals by 1000, simply move the decimal point <u>three</u> places to the <u>RIGHT</u> because there are three zeros in 1<u>000</u>.

    Ex:

    42.6 × 1000 = 42,600

    42.6⁰⁰ = 42,600

    Ex:

    0.920 × 1000 = 920

    0.920.   (zero and decimal point on far left goes away to equal 920)

Multiplying Decimals by Whole Numbers or a Decimal

Unlike adding and subtracting decimals, you do <u>NOT</u> line up the decimal points under each other. The placement of the decimal point in the product depends on how many digits are on the right in the problem.

Ex:

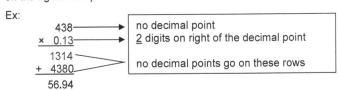

Since there are only <u>two</u> digits on the right in the problem, the decimal point must be put so that there are only <u>two</u> digits on the right in the product.

Ex:

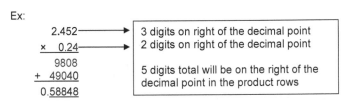

* <u>Note</u> – one zero <u>MUST</u> go on the left side of the decimal point because there is <u>NO</u> whole number in the product.

Ex:

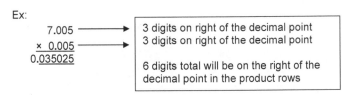

To have 6 digits on the right of the decimal point, you must add zeros to the <u>LEFT</u> in the product.

Ex:

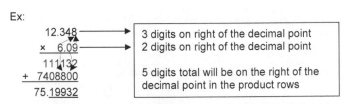

* <u>Note</u> – do <u>NOT</u> put a row of zeros, just bring the zero down (red zero) and then proceed to multiply by 6. There are five digits (see underline marks) on the right side of the decimal point in the product.

Chapter 5:

DIVISION

$32 \div 8 = 4$

- students in all
- students per lunch table
- tables needed

divisor 8)32 4 Quotient / dividend
             32
              0 remainder

Division

Division is the process of putting a large amount into groups that all have equal amounts.

Ex:

20 ÷ 4 = 5

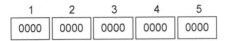

Twenty divided by four means that 4 will be in each group, therefore, 5 groups are made up with 4 in each group to equal 20.

Parts of a division problem:

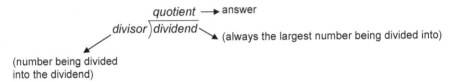

So the dividend is divided by the divisor to get the quotient.

Ex:

$$4\overline{)20}^{\,5}$$

Any number left over at the end becomes the remainder and is put at the top in the quotient after the letter R.

You are going to use your basic multiplication facts when dividing.

Steps of Division

Step 1: Divide

```
      1
   _____
6 ) 816
```

Ask yourself if 6 (divisor) will go into 8, yes, 1 time so, 1 goes above the 8 in the quotient.

Step 2: Multiply
 $1 \times 6 = 6$
 6 goes right under the 8

```
      1
   _____
6 ) 816
   6
```

Step 3: Subtract
 $8 - 6 = 2$
 2 goes under the line

```
      1
   _____
6 ) 816
   -6
   ___
    2
```

Step 4: Check (√) to be sure that the number you got when you subtracted is LESS than the divisor. 2 is <u>less</u> than 6, which tells you automatically that the 1 in the quotient is <u>CORRECT</u>.

* <u>Note</u> – at this stage of the problem, NOTHING goes under the 16. You are only dealing with the 8.

Step 5: Bring down

Bring down the next number in the dividend next to the number you got when you subtracted.

```
      1
   _____
6 ) 816
   -6↓
   ___
   21
```

Now repeat all steps.

Step 1: Divide
 21 ÷ 6 = 3
 Put 3 in the quotient above the 1

```
      13
   _____
 6 ) 816
    -6
    ___
     21
```

Step 2: Multiply
 3 × 6 = 18
 Put 18 under 21

```
      13
   _____
 6 ) 816
    -6
    ___
     21
    -18
```

Step 3: Subtract
 21 − 18 = 3
 Put 3 under the line

```
      13
   _____
 6 ) 816
    -6
    ___
     21
    -18
    ___
      3
```

Step 4: Check (√) is 3 less than 6? Yes.

Step 5: Bring Down
Bring down the 6 in the dividend and put it next to the 3

Now repeat all steps.

Step 1: Divide
36 ÷ 6 = 6
Put 6 above the 6 in the quotient

```
      136
   6 ) 816
      -6
       21
      -18
       36
```

Step 2: Multiply
6 × 6 = 36
Put 36 under 36

```
      136
   6 ) 816
      -6
       21
      -18
       36
       36
```

Step 3: Subtract
36 − 36 = 0

```
      136
   6 ) 816
      -6
       21
      -18
       36
     - 36
        0
```

Step 4: Check (√) is 0 less than 6? Yes.

* <u>Note</u> – Remember you <u>MUST</u> check to make sure the number you get when you subtract <u>MUST</u> be <u>LESS</u> than your divisor. This tells you that you've done the steps correctly.

If your remainder is greater than the divisor, you MUST change the number you put in the quotient and do all the steps again.

Ex:

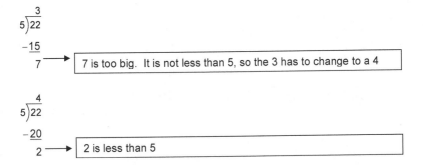

All steps are repeated until there are no more numbers to bring down.

To ensure that you are doing all the steps in the correct order, put the following signs at the top right of your paper:

÷
×
-
√
↓

No matter how large the dividend and the divisor numbers are, the same steps are followed until there are no more numbers to bring down.

It is helpful to use graph paper to practice on to make sure all numbers are in their proper place.

In the following problem, note that nothing goes over the 3 because 7 won't go into 3, but it will go into 34, so the first number must go above the 4 in the quotient.

Ex:

÷
×
-
√
↓

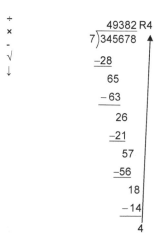

4 is the final remainder. There are <u>no</u> more numbers to bring down and 4 is <u>less</u> than 7.

The 4 goes at the top at the end of the quotient after a capital R for remainder.

Final complete answer is 49,382 R4.

If you don't bring the remainder up to the quotient, the answer won't be correct. It will be incomplete.

To check a division problem, multiply the quotient times the divisor to get the dividend and <u>add</u> the remainder, if you have one.

```
  49,382
×      7
```
345,674 + 4 = 345,678   Check (√)

Division by Two Digits in the Divisor

All the same division steps are followed.

The <u>FIRST</u> thing you must do is decide where the <u>first</u> number goes in the quotient.

Ex:

Step 1 – <u>Divide</u>

```
        8
  42)3415
```

Ask yourself if 42 will go into 3.
NO, so <u>NOTHING</u> can go over 3.
Will 42 go into 34?
NO, so <u>NOTHING</u> can go over the 4.
Will 42 go into 341? <u>YES</u>, so the first number goes above 1.
To figure out what the number is going to be look at the digit in the tens place in the divisor and underline it. Ask yourself how many times 4 will go into 34 (4 won't go into 3 but it will go into 34). It will go into 34 eight times. Put 8 above the 1 in the quotient.

* <u>Note</u> – say to yourself, I don't know my 42 times tables, but I do know my 4's, so you are only going to use the 4 for the dividing step.

Step 2: <u>Multiply</u>

    42 x 8 = 336
    Put 336 under 341

```
        8
  42)3415
   -336
```

* <u>Note</u> – You MUST ALWAYS multiply the number you put in the quotient by the <u>WHOLE</u> divisor, 8 × 42, not just the 4

Step 3: <u>Subtract</u>

    341 – 336 = 5

```
        8
  42)3415
   -336
      5
```

Step 4: Check (√) is 5 less than 42? Yes.

Step 5: Bring down

Bring down the 5 in the dividend down next to the 5

```
        8
42)3415
   -336↓
      55
```

Now repeat all Steps.

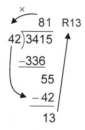

Step 1: Divide 42 into 55 = 1
Step 2: Multiply 1 × 42 = 42. Put the 42 under the 55
Step 3: Subtract 55 − 42 = 13
Step 4: Check (√), is 13 less than 42? Yes
Step 5: 13 is the remainder, as there is no more numbers to bring down

Dividing by Three Digits in the Divisor

Follow all the same steps.

Step 1: Divide
234 will NOT go into 5 or 56 but it will go in to 568, so the first number goes over the 8. Only use the 2 and 5 to get that number 5 ÷ 2 = 2

```
        2
2̲34)5687
```

Step 2: Multiply
234 × 2 = 468
Put 468 under 568

```
   x
  ↙‾‾‾
       2
234)5687
  - 468
```

* Note – you must always multiply the WHOLE divisor by the number you put in the quotient.

Step 3: Subtract
568 – 468 = 100

```
        2
234)5687
  - 468
    100
```

Step 4: Check (√) is 100 less than 234? Yes.

Step 5: Bring down

Bring down the 7 down next to 100

```
         2
    234)5687
       -468↓
        1007
```

Now repeat all Steps.

Step 1: Divide
Only use the 2 in the divisor into the 10 (see underlines) 10 ÷ 2 = 5

BUT if we multiply 5 × 234 = 1170, this is too big. You can NOT subtract 1170 from 1007, so 5 must go down to a 4. Put the 4 above the 7.

```
         24
    234)5687
       -468
        1007
```

Step 2: Multiply
    234 × 4 = 936

```
         24
    234)5687
       -468
        1007
        -936
```

Step 3 : Subtract
1007 − 936 = 71

```
         24
   234)5687
      − 468
       1007
       −936
         71
```

Step 4 – Check (√) is 71 less than 234? Yes.

Step 5 – There are no more numbers to bring down, so 71 becomes the remainder.

```
         24   R71
   234)5687  ↑
      − 468
       1007
       −936
         71
```

Whole answer is 24 R 71

Zeros in the Quotient

If after you bring down in Step 5 and you can't divide, but there are more numbers to bring down in the dividend, a zero is put up in the quotient above the number that you brought down. Then bring the next number down. Now you can do all the steps again.

Ex:

```
       2
   ┌──────
21 )4214
    -42↓
    ────
      01
```

| 21 will not go into 1 |

```
      20
   ┌──────
21 )4214
    -42 ↓
    ────
      14
```

| Put a zero (0) above the 1 in the dividend and then bring the 4 down to the 1 |

```
     200
   ┌──────
21 )4214
    -42
    ────
      14
```

| 21 will not go into 14 so another zero (0) must be put above the 4 in the dividend |

```
     200R14
   ┌──────
21 )4214
    -42
    ────
      14
```

| There are no more numbers to bring down so the 14 becomes the remainder |

Ex:

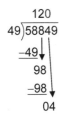

49 will not go into 4 so a zero (0) goes above the 4 in the dividend

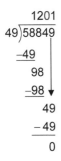

Bring the 9 down

49 ÷ 49 = 1
Put 1 on top of the 9

49 × 1 = 49
Put 49 under 49

Subtract 49 − 49 = 0

No remainder

Dividing Whole Numbers into Decimals

All the same steps are followed. The decimal point MUST be brought directly up into the quotient BEFORE you start to do any of the steps. If you don't, there's a chance you will forget to put it in later. If you leave it out, even if you have the correct numbers, it will be wrong.

If after you divide in step 1 and there is NO whole number on the left side of the decimal point, you MUST put one zero on the left side of the decimal point.

Ex:

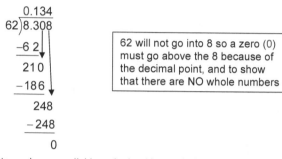

62 will not go into 8 so a zero (0) must go above the 8 because of the decimal point, and to show that there are NO whole numbers

* Note – when you divide a decimal by a whole number, your answer is ALWAYS a decimal number.

Dividing Money

Follow all the same dividing steps.

<u>Before</u> dividing, put the dollar sign and decimal point up in the quotient so they don't get left out.

$$\overline{\smash{\big)}\$\,.}^{\$\,.}$$

Ex:

```
       $ 2.55
    5)$12.75
      −10
       27
      −25
        25
       −25
         0
```

When dividing a whole number into money, your answer is <u>ALWAYS</u> money.

When dividing money into money, your answer will <u>NEVER</u> be money, it will be a whole number.

Ex:

If you are asked how many quarters are in $6.75, you are dividing money into money. Your answer will be a whole number, the amount of quarters.

$0.25\overline{)\$6.75}$

You must change the decimal number in the divisor to a whole number before you can divide. To do this, you move the decimal point to the <u>RIGHT</u> in the divisor, all the way to the right, so that you form a whole number, $ 0.25. = 25. Since you moved it two places, you MUST also move the decimal point in the dividend two places to the right, $ 6.75 = 675

$0.25\overline{)\$6.75}$ 27.   (whole number)

<u>NO</u> dollar sign ($) goes in the quotient. Put the decimal point in the new place.

Answer – There are 27 quarters in $6.75.

Dividing Decimals into Decimals

When dividing decimals into decimals, just like money but regular decimals, you do the same thing by moving the decimal points.

Ex:

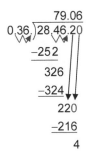

We moved the decimal point to the <u>RIGHT</u> in the divisor, so we must move the decimal point to the right in the dividend

Bring the decimal point up into the quotient, into the new place.

Do all the steps

* <u>Note</u> – we added a zero (**0**) in the dividend to bring down next to the 4 so we could continue to divide. We would need to add more zeros, but it still will not come out even so you can stop. There will be a remainder or you can round it to specific decimal place.

Decimal Patterns in Division by 10; 100; 1000; etc.

Remember when we multiplied by 10, 100, or 1000, we simply moved the decimal point to the right according to the number of zeros.

In division the decimal point moves to the LEFT according to the number of zeros.

When you divide by 1<u>0</u>, simply move the decimal point <u>one</u> place to its LEFT because there is <u>one</u> zero in 1<u>0</u>.

Ex:
$$6.483 \div 10 = 0.6483$$

When you divide by 1<u>00</u>, simply move the decimal point <u>two</u> places to the LEFT because there are <u>two</u> zeros in 1<u>00</u>.

Ex:
$$6.483 \div 100 = 0.06483$$

When you divide by 1<u>000</u>, simply move the decimal point <u>three</u> places to the LEFT because there are <u>three</u> zeros in 1<u>000</u>.

Ex:
$$0.8 \div 1000 = 0.0008$$

* <u>Note</u> - notice we had to add zeros to the left of the numbers to put the decimal point in the correct spot.

Every whole number has a decimal point on the right even if we don't see it. Think of money, five dollars can be written as $5.00 or $5.

So when you divide a whole number by 1<u>00</u>, simply move the decimal point <u>two</u> places to the <u>LEFT</u> because there are <u>two</u> zeros in 1<u>00</u>.

Ex:

14 ÷ 100 = 0.14

Proof!

$$\begin{array}{r} 0.14 \\ 100\overline{)14.00} \\ -100 \\ \hline 400 \\ -400 \\ \hline 0 \end{array}$$

| Put the decimal point right of the 14 |
| Bring up the decimal point into the quotient |
| Add zero's so you can divide |

Ex:

6,483 ÷ 100 = 0.06483

$$\begin{array}{r} 0.06483 \\ 100\overline{)6.48300} \\ -600 \\ \hline 483 \\ -400 \\ \hline 830 \\ -800 \\ \hline 300 \\ -300 \\ \hline 0 \end{array}$$

* <u>Note</u> – we needed to add two zero's in the dividend to continue dividing.

82

Divisibility
Rules of Divisibility

1. ALL even numbers are divisible by 2.

2. ALL numbers that end in 5 or 0 are divisible by 5.

   Ex: 15 ÷ 5 = 3

   Ex: 20 ÷ 5 = 4

3. ALL numbers that end in 0 are divisible by 2, 5, and 10.

   Ex: 10 ÷ 2 = 5   10 ÷ 5 = 2   10 ÷ 10 = 1
       20 ÷ 2 = 10   20 ÷ 5 = 2   20 ÷ 10 = 2
       40 ÷ 2 = 20   40 ÷ 5 = 8   40 ÷ 10 = 4

4. Any product whose digits add up to a number that can be divided by 3, is divisible by 3.

   Ex: 354 is divisible by 3

   Add the digits 3 + 5 + 4 = 12

   12 can be divided by 3, therefore; 354 is divisible by 3

Proof!
$$\begin{array}{r} 118 \\ 3\overline{)354} \\ \underline{-3} \\ 5 \\ \underline{-3} \\ 24 \\ \underline{-24} \\ 0 \end{array}$$

5. If a number is divisible by both 2 and 3, it is automatically divisible by 6.

   Ex: 24 is divisible by 2 = 12

   Ex: 24 is divisible by 3 = 8

   So, it is automatically divisible by 6.   24 ÷ 6 = 4

   Ex: 354 is divisible by 2 because it is <u>even</u>, = 177

   It is divisible by 3 = 118

   So it is automatically divisible by 6 = 59

Proof!
$$\begin{array}{r} 59 \\ 6\overline{)354} \\ \underline{-30} \\ 54 \\ \underline{-54} \\ 0 \end{array}$$

Estimating Quotients

When you estimate quotients, you must think of your basic times table facts for the number you are dividing by. You must come CLOSEST to the number you are dividing into.

Ex:

$\overline{60}$
$6\overline{)357}$
360

Think of the 6 times tables
6 × 5 = 30, 6 × 6 = 36
36 is CLOSEST to 35
So 357 becomes 360

$\overline{40}$
$9\overline{)388}$
360

Think of the 9 times tables
9 × 3 = 27, 9 × 4 = 36, 9 × 5 = 45
36 is CLOSEST to 38
So 388 becomes 360

$\overline{400}$
$7\overline{)2983}$
2800

Think of the 7 times tables
7 × 3 = 21, 7 × 4 = 28, 7 × 5 = 35
28 is CLOSEST to 29
So 2983 becomes 2800

$\overline{400}$
$11\overline{)4263}$
4400

Think of the 11 times tables
11 × 3 = 33, 11 × 4 = 44
44 is CLOSEST to 42
So 4263 becomes 4400

$\overline{60}$
$28\overline{)1953}$
301800

Round 28 to 30
Think of the 3 times tables
3 × 6 = 18, 3 × 7 = 21
18 is CLOSEST to 19
So 1953 becomes 1800

$$\begin{array}{r}90\\\underline{4}37\overline{)35{,}847}\\\underline{4}0036{,}000\end{array}$$

> Round 437 to 400
>
> Think of the 4 times tables
> $4 \times 8 = 32$, $\underline{4 \times 9 = 36}$
>
> 36 is <u>CLOSEST</u> to 35
> So 35,847 becomes 36,000

Interpreting Remainders

Division word problems may present a question that will not be any of the numbers you get when you divide for the answer. You may have to change the quotient or the question may ask for the remainder for the answer.

Ex:

A class of 26 needs to order binders for the class. The binders come in boxes of 8. How many boxes should be ordered?

(binders per box) $8\overline{)26}$ students $\;\;\;$ quotient: 3 full boxes, remainder 2 students $\;\;\;$ 4 boxes are needed

3 in the quotient will give only 24 students binders. 2 students are left that won't get one, so another box needs to be ordered so every student gets one.

Ex:

166 fifth graders are going on a field trip. One bus holds 64 students. How many buses will be needed?

<u>3</u> buses needed

(students per bus) $64\overline{)166}$ students $\;\;\;$ quotient: 2 full buses, remainder 38 students $\;\;\;$ 3 buses are needed

2 buses will carry only 128 students. 38 students can't go if they don't have another bus. You may be one of the 38 and I know that you want to go.

Ex:

842 students order lunch every day. Milk cartons are ordered by the crate holding 150. If enough cartons are ordered, how many cartons will be left over for the next day?

<u>58</u> cartons left over

```
                              5 full crates
(cartons per crate)    150 )‾842 students         6 crates need to be ordered
                             -750
                              92 students
```

```
150   cartons per crate      900    total cartons
×  6  crates                - 842   students
900   cartons                 58    cartons left over for next day
```

Order of Operations

$(3 \times 4) + 2$ or $3 \times (4 + 2)$

Both of these have the same numbers and operational signs but they are grouped differently. Does it matter? Yes.

If you do what is in parentheses first in each problem, you do not get the same answers.

Ex:

$(3 \times 4) + 2$ or $3 \times (4 + 2)$
$12 + 2 = 14$ $3 \times 6 = 18$

Two different answers.

When doing these types of problems, follow the following steps:

1. Always multiply and/or divide first from left to right.

2. Then add and/or subtract from left to right.

So the above problem at the left is done correctly.

Ex:

$(14 \div 2) + (3 \times 5) - 2 =$
$\quad (7 \ + \ 15) \ - 2 =$
$\qquad\quad 22 \ \ -2 =$
$\qquad\qquad 20$

If a problem is presented with parentheses and/or exponents, do these FIRST, then do the remaining operations in order given.

Ex:

$10 \div (3 + 2) \times 4 - 3 =$
$10 \div \ \ 5 \ \ \ \times 4 - 3 =$
$\quad\ \ 2 \quad \times 4 - 3 =$
$\qquad\quad\ \ 8 \ \ - 3 =$
$\qquad\qquad\ \ 5$

Chapter 6:

FRACTIONS

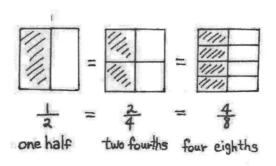

Fractions

Fractions show parts of a whole number. When a whole number is divided into equal parts, a fraction can be made using a certain number of parts. All parts MUST be equal in size to make fractions.

Ex:

▪ = 1 whole

☐ = 2 equal parts, <u>each</u> part is $\frac{1}{2}$

A fraction is written as one number over another with a <u>straight</u> line in between them. Do <u>not</u> make a slanted line.

Parts of a fraction -- 1 = numerator
2 = denominator

The **denominator** always tells how many TOTAL parts there are.

The **numerator** tells how many of the total parts you are talking about.

Ex:
$\frac{3}{4}$ - parts shaded
- total parts

A number line can also show fractions as on a ruler, parts of an inch.

Ex:

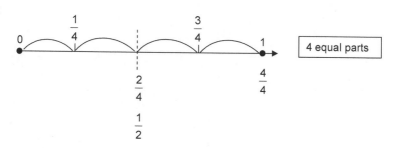

4 equal parts

As you can see $\frac{4}{4}$ equals 1 whole. When the numerator and denominator are the same number, it <u>ALWAYS</u> equals 1 whole, no matter what the numbers are.

Ex:

$$\frac{10}{10}=1 \quad \frac{24}{24}=1 \quad \frac{159}{159}=1$$

When the numerator is <u>smaller</u> than the denominator, this makes a **proper fraction**.

When the numerator is <u>larger</u> than the denominator, this makes an **improper fraction**.

Equivalent Decimals and Fractions

HUNDRETHS

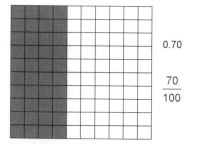
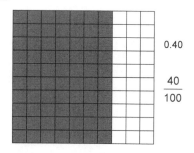

TENTHS

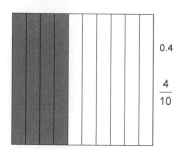
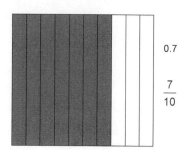

$0.40 = 0.4^0$ $0.70 = 0.7^0$

$$\frac{40}{100} = \frac{4}{10}$$ $$\frac{70}{100} = \frac{7}{10}$$

Here you can see that they are equal in the amount that is shaded. This is why you can drop the zero on the far right without changing the value.

Equivalent Fractions

Equivalent fractions represent the same amount or value.

Ex:

$$\frac{1}{2}=\frac{2}{4}=\frac{3}{6}=\frac{4}{8}=\frac{5}{10}=\frac{6}{12}$$

Proof!

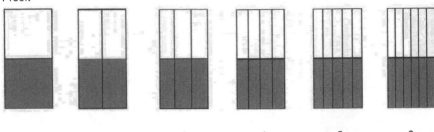

$$\frac{1}{2} = \frac{2}{4} = \frac{3}{6} = \frac{4}{8} = \frac{5}{10} = \frac{6}{12}$$

As you can see, each represents the <u>SAME</u> amount shaded but, each is divided in different amounts of equal parts.

To find an equivalent fraction, simply multiply or divide <u>BOTH</u> numerator <u>AND</u> denominator by the <u>SAME</u> number.

Ex:

$$\frac{1^{\times 2}}{2_{\times 2}}=\frac{2}{4} \qquad \frac{1^{\times 3}}{2_{\times 3}}=\frac{3}{6} \qquad \frac{1^{\times 4}}{2_{\times 4}}=\frac{4}{8}$$

$$\frac{15^{\div 5}}{30_{\div 5}}=\frac{3}{6} \qquad \frac{15^{\div 3}}{30_{\div 3}}=\frac{5}{10}$$

Other equivalent fractions:

$$\frac{1}{3}=\frac{2}{6}=\frac{3}{9}=\frac{4}{12}=\frac{5}{15}=\frac{6}{18}=\frac{7}{21}=\frac{8}{24}=\frac{9}{27}$$

$$\frac{1}{4}=\frac{2}{8}=\frac{3}{12}=\frac{4}{16}=\frac{5}{20}=\frac{6}{24}=\frac{7}{28}=\frac{8}{32}=\frac{9}{36}$$

$$\frac{1}{5}=\frac{2}{10}=\frac{3}{15}=\frac{4}{20}=\frac{5}{25}=\frac{6}{30}=\frac{7}{35}=\frac{8}{40}=\frac{9}{45}$$

$$\frac{1}{6}=\frac{2}{12}=\frac{3}{18}=\frac{4}{24}=\frac{5}{30}=\frac{6}{36}=\frac{7}{42}=\frac{8}{48}=\frac{9}{54}$$

$$\frac{1}{7}=\frac{2}{14}=\frac{3}{21}=\frac{4}{28}=\frac{5}{35}=\frac{6}{42}=\frac{7}{49}=\frac{8}{56}=\frac{9}{63}$$

$$\frac{1}{8}=\frac{2}{16}=\frac{3}{24}=\frac{4}{32}=\frac{5}{40}=\frac{6}{48}=\frac{7}{56}=\frac{8}{64}=\frac{9}{72}$$

$$\frac{1}{9}=\frac{2}{18}=\frac{3}{27}=\frac{4}{36}=\frac{5}{45}=\frac{6}{54}=\frac{7}{63}=\frac{8}{72}=\frac{9}{81}$$

If you are asked to find a missing numerator or denominator in a set of equivalent fractions, look at the parts that are already there. Decide if they multiplied or divided to get the other number.

Ex:

$$\frac{2}{8} = \frac{6}{?}$$

Look at the 2 and the 6
2 × 3 = 6
Do the SAME thing to the 8
8 × 3 = 24

$$\frac{2^{\times 3}}{8_{\times 3}} = \frac{6}{24}$$

Ex:

$$\frac{28}{35} = \frac{?}{5}$$

Look at the 35 and the 5
35 ÷ 7 = 5
Do the SAME thing to the 28
28 ÷ 7 = 4

$$\frac{28^{\div 7}}{35_{\div 7}} = \frac{4}{5}$$

Simplest Form (SF)

Simplest form, also known as reducing to lowest terms, is when a fraction is put into its most basic terms, smallest equivalent fraction.

To do this, find the Greatest Common Factor (GCF), and divide that number into <u>BOTH</u> the numerator and the denominator. You are making the smallest equivalent fractions.

Ex:

$$\frac{12^{\div 4}}{16_{\div 4}} = \frac{3}{4}$$

4 is the GCF. It is the greatest number that can go into <u>BOTH</u> 12 and 16. This gives you a fraction that can NOT get any smaller. No single number can go into <u>BOTH</u> 3 and 4 to make them <u>smaller</u>.

Ex:

$$\frac{10^{\div 5}}{15_{\div 5}} = \frac{2}{3} \qquad \frac{18^{\div 6}}{24_{\div 6}} = \frac{3}{4}$$

If you don't get the simplest form the first time, you may need to reduce it again by dividing it by a new GCF.

Ex:

2 Steps:
$$\frac{18^{\div 2}}{24_{\div 2}} = \frac{9^{\div 3}}{12_{\div 3}} = \frac{3}{4} \qquad \frac{42^{\div 2}}{66_{\div 2}} = \frac{21^{\div 3}}{33_{\div 3}} = \frac{7}{11}$$

1 Step:
$$\frac{18^{\div 6}}{24_{\div 6}} = \frac{3}{4} \qquad \frac{42^{\div 6}}{66_{\div 6}} = \frac{7}{11}$$

* <u>Note</u> – you should always look to see if the numerator will go into the denominator evenly. If it will, than the numerator is automatically the GCF and will be used to find the simplest form.

Ex:

$$\frac{8^{\div 8}}{24_{\div 8}} = \frac{1}{3}$$

8 will go evenly into 24 so 8 is the GCF.
Divide: 8 ÷ 8 = 1
24 ÷ 8 = 3

* <u>Note</u> – the number you divide by will <u>**NEVER**</u> be larger than the numerator.

Least Common Denominator (LCD)

To find the Least Common Denominator (LCD) for two or more fractions, you find the least common multiple. They are the same thing.

Ex:

$$\frac{3^{\times 3}}{4_{\times 3}} = \frac{9}{12}$$

$$\frac{5^{\times 2}}{6_{\times 2}} = \frac{10}{12}$$

> For denominators, we have a 4 and 6
>
> List the multiples for each:
>
> 4 = 4, 8, ⑫, 16, 20, 24...
>
> 6 = 6, ⑫, 18, 24...
>
> 12 is the LCD
>
> Then find equivalent fractions

When we add and subtract fractions with different denominators, you must find the LCD and make equivalent fractions with the <u>SAME</u> denominators before you can add or subtract.

Comparing Fractions

If two fractions have the <u>SAME</u> denominators, simply compare the numerators.

Ex:

$$\frac{3}{4} > \frac{1}{4}$$ 3 is greater than 1

$$\frac{2}{7} < \frac{5}{7}$$ 2 is less than 5

Comparing fractions with different denominators can be done in two ways, a long way and a short cut way.

<u>LONG WAY</u> –

First, find the LCD to make new equivalent fractions that have the same denominator, then compare.

Ex:

Step 1: Find the LCD by thinking of the <u>FIRST</u> number that <u>both</u> denominators can go into. 2 and 8 can go into 8 so the LCD is 8

$$\frac{1}{2} \qquad \frac{7}{8}$$

$$\frac{}{8} \qquad \frac{}{8}$$

* <u>Note</u> – you are making equivalent fractions.

Step 2: Divide 2 into 8 = 4
Multiply 1 ÷ 4 = 4
4 makes the new numerator

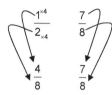

If the denominator stays the same, the numerator stays the same. $\frac{7}{8}$ is just brought down.

Compare the new fractions, $\frac{4}{8}$ is less than $\frac{7}{8}$

Step 3: The original fractions get the <

$$\frac{1}{2} < \frac{7}{8}$$

Ex:

Step 1: Find the LCD for 8 and 6. 24 is the <u>FIRST</u> number that both 8 and 6 can go into. So 24 is the LCD.

$$\frac{7}{8} \qquad \frac{5}{6}$$

$$\frac{}{24} \qquad \frac{}{24}$$

Step 2: Divide old denominators into 24.

$24 \div 8 = \underline{3} \quad 24 \div 6 = \underline{4}$

Multiply by the old numerator to get the new numerators.

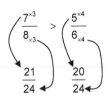

$$\left(\frac{7^{\times 3}}{8_{\times 3}}\right) > \left(\frac{5^{\times 4}}{6_{\times 4}}\right)$$

$$\frac{21}{24} \quad \frac{20}{24}$$

21 is greater than 20. Compare.

Comparing Fractions

Short Cut

Another, quicker way to compare fractions is simply to cross multiply <u>diagonally</u> to get two numbers to compare.

Ex:

Multiply 1 × 8 = 8, put 8 above 1,
Multiply 2 × 7 = 14, put 14 above 7, now 8 is less than 14, so less sign is used

$$\frac{1}{2} < \frac{7}{8}$$

Ex:

$$\overset{42}{\frac{7}{8}} > \overset{40}{\frac{5}{6}} \qquad \begin{array}{l} 7 \times 6 = 42 \\ 8 \times 5 = 40 \end{array}$$

$$\overset{15}{\frac{5}{8}} < \overset{16}{\frac{2}{3}} \qquad \begin{array}{l} 5 \times 3 = 15 \\ 2 \times 8 = 16 \end{array}$$

$$\overset{18}{\frac{6}{7}} > \overset{14}{\frac{2}{3}} \qquad \begin{array}{l} 6 \times 3 = 18 \\ 2 \times 7 = 14 \end{array}$$

$$\overset{36}{\frac{4}{7}} > \overset{28}{\frac{4}{9}} \qquad \begin{array}{l} 4 \times 9 = 36 \\ 7 \times 4 = 28 \end{array}$$

If both numerators are 1 and the denominators are different, the <u>larger</u> denominator is <u>ALWAYS</u> the smaller fraction.

Ex:

$$\frac{1}{5} > \frac{1}{7}$$

7 is the larger denominator so $\frac{1}{7}$ is less than $\frac{1}{5}$

Ordering Fractions

When putting fractions with the same denominators in order, simply arrange them by the numerator according to the directions for least (**L**) to greatest (**G**) or greatest (**G**) to least (**L**). Pay very close attention to the directions.

Ex: Order fractions from least to greatest.

$$\frac{2}{12} \quad \frac{6}{12} \quad \frac{4}{12} \quad \frac{8}{12} \quad \frac{1}{12}$$

> Since all of the denominators are the same, just look at the numerator

$$\frac{1}{12} \quad \frac{2}{12} \quad \frac{4}{12} \quad \frac{6}{12} \quad \frac{8}{12}$$

When the denominators are different, you **MUST** first make equivalent fractions that all have the **SAME** denominators, and then put in order.

Ex: Order fractions from least to greatest.

Step 1: Looking at all of the denominators below, find the LCD. 24 is the first number that all of the denominators can go into, so 24 is the LCD.

$$\frac{3}{6} \quad \frac{2}{3} \quad \frac{1}{6} \quad \frac{7}{12} \quad \frac{5}{8}$$

$$\frac{}{24} \quad \frac{}{24} \quad \frac{}{24} \quad \frac{}{24} \quad \frac{}{24}$$

Step 2: Find the equivalent number for each.

$$\frac{3^{\times 4}}{6_{\times 4}} \quad \frac{2^{\times 8}}{3_{\times 8}} \quad \frac{1^{\times 4}}{6_{\times 4}} \quad \frac{7^{\times 2}}{12_{\times 2}} \quad \frac{5^{\times 3}}{8_{\times 3}}$$

$$\frac{12}{24} \quad \frac{16}{24} \quad \frac{4}{24} \quad \frac{14}{24} \quad \frac{15}{24}$$

Step 3: Arrange new fraction in order from least to greatest.

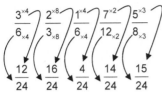

Step 4: Match up the ORIGINAL fractions for each correct order.

$$\frac{1}{6} \quad \frac{3}{6} \quad \frac{7}{12} \quad \frac{5}{8} \quad \frac{2}{3}$$

Final Answer

Ex: Order fractions from greatest to least.

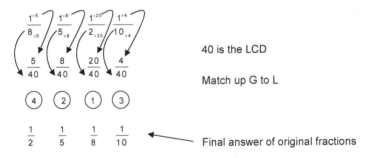

40 is the LCD

Match up G to L

Final answer of original fractions

* <u>Note</u> – remember, if all numerators are 1, the largest denominator is the smallest; the smallest denominator is the largest.

Ex:

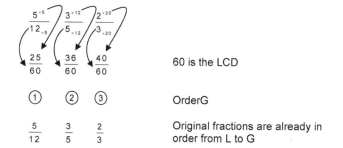

60 is the LCD

OrderG

Original fractions are already in order from L to G

Ex:

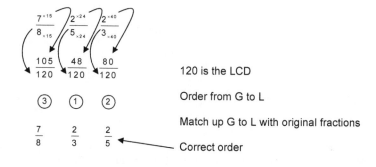

120 is the LCD

Order from G to L

Match up G to L with original fractions

Correct order

Ordering Fraction and Decimal Combinations

When you have a combination of fractions and decimals to put in order, you <u>MUST</u> change them to all fractions or all decimals.

Every decimal can be written as a fraction. If you have a decimal in the tenths place, it has a 10 as the denominator.

Ex:

    0.4   You read this as four tenths

    $\dfrac{4}{10}$ You read this as four tenths

If you have a decimal in the hundredths place, it has a 100 as the denominator.

Ex:

    0.25   You read this as twenty-five hundredths

    $\dfrac{25}{100}$ You read this as twenty-five hundredths

If you have a decimal in the thousandths place, it has a 1000 as a denominator.

Ex:

    0.342   You read this as three hundred forty-two thousandths

    $\dfrac{342}{1000}$ You read this as three hundred forty-two thousandths

Change the following to all <u>fractions</u> and put in order from L to G.

Ex:

$0.5 \quad \dfrac{3}{5} \quad 0.9 \quad \dfrac{1}{3} \quad \dfrac{1}{6}$

$\dfrac{5}{10}^{\times 3}_{\times 3} \quad \dfrac{3}{5}^{\times 6}_{\times 6} \quad \dfrac{9}{10}^{\times 3}_{\times 3} \quad \dfrac{1}{3}^{\times 10}_{\times 10} \quad \dfrac{1}{6}^{\times 5}_{\times 5}$

$\dfrac{15}{30} \quad \dfrac{18}{30} \quad \dfrac{27}{30} \quad \dfrac{10}{30} \quad \dfrac{5}{30}$

③ ④ ⑤ ② ①

| Now, find the LCD for the group 30 is the LCD |
| Find the equivalent numerator |
| Put new fractions in order from L to G |

$\dfrac{1}{6} \quad \dfrac{1}{3} \quad 0.5 \quad \dfrac{3}{5} \quad 0.9$

Match new fractions with original group

Change original group to all <u>decimals</u>.

Same Order

$0.5 \quad \dfrac{3}{5} \quad 0.9 \quad \dfrac{1}{3} \quad \dfrac{1}{6}$

$0.5^{00} \quad 0.6^{00} \quad 0.9^{00} \quad 0.33^{0} \quad 0.166$
↑ ↑ ↑ ↑ ↑
$\dfrac{1}{6} \quad \dfrac{1}{3} \quad 0.5 \quad \dfrac{3}{5} \quad 0.9$

③ ④ ⑤ ② ①

| Original Group |
| Changed to decimals |
| (add magic zero's) |
| Match to original group (same order) |
| Order L to G |

To change fractions to decimals that do NOT have a 10, 100, or 1000 as the denominator, you must divide the denominator into the numerator.

Ex:

$$\frac{3}{5} = 0.6 \quad \begin{array}{r} 0.6 \\ 5\overline{)3.0} \\ \underline{3\ 0} \\ 0 \end{array}$$

$$\frac{1}{3} = 0.33 \quad \begin{array}{r} 0.33 \\ 3\overline{)1.00} \\ \underline{9} \\ 10 \\ \underline{9} \\ 1 \end{array}$$

$$\frac{1}{6} = 0.166 \quad \begin{array}{r} 0.166 \\ 6\overline{)1.000} \\ \underline{6} \\ 40 \\ \underline{36} \\ 40 \\ \underline{36} \\ 4 \end{array}$$

* Note – Remember, every whole number has a decimal point on its right. When dividing a large whole number into a smaller whole number, put the decimal point after the whole number in the dividend and add zeros, then divide. This will give you a decimal answer in the quotient.

Adding and Subtracting Fractions

When you add or subtract fractions with the SAME denominator simply add or subtract the numerators. If necessary, you ALWAYS put final answer in simplest form for it to be complete and correct.

Ex:

$$\begin{array}{r}\dfrac{1}{6}\\+\dfrac{3}{6}\\\hline\dfrac{4^{\div2}}{6_{\div2}}=\dfrac{2}{3}\end{array}$$

You only add the numerators. The denominator does NOT change.

$\dfrac{4}{6}$ is not in simplest form, so you must find the greatest number that will go into BOTH 4 and 6 to make them the smallest that they can go. 2 is the only number that will go into both.

Ex:

$$\begin{array}{r}\dfrac{6}{10}\\-\dfrac{3}{10}\\\hline\dfrac{3}{10}\end{array}$$

The fraction $\dfrac{3}{10}$ is already in simplest form.

No number can go into BOTH to make them smaller, so $\dfrac{3}{10}$ is the final answer.

When you add or subtract fractions with <u>DIFFERENT</u> denominators, you must first make new equivalent fractions with the <u>SAME</u> denominator. Then you can add or subtract. Remember to put the final answer in simplest form.

Ex:

$$\frac{1^{\times 3}}{6_{\times 3}} = \frac{3}{18}$$

$$+\frac{2^{\times 2}}{9_{\times 2}} = \frac{4}{18}$$

$$\frac{7}{18}$$

18 is the LCD for both 6 and 9

Find equivalent numerators, and then add

$\frac{7}{18}$ is the answer, it is already in simplest form.

* <u>Note</u> – Nothing goes under the original set of fractions.

Ex:

$$\frac{7^{\times 4}}{9_{\times 4}} = \frac{28}{36}$$

$$-\frac{3^{\times 9}}{4_{\times 9}} = \frac{27}{36}$$

$$\frac{1}{36}$$

36 is the LCD for 9 and 4

Ex:

$$\frac{7}{12} \rightarrow \frac{7}{12}$$

$$-\frac{1^{\times 4}}{3_{\times 4}} = \frac{4}{12}$$

$$\frac{3}{12} = \frac{1}{4}$$

12 is the LCD so it is the first fraction that comes over

The fraction, $\frac{3}{12}$, is not in simplest form so it must be reduced to its lowest terms

112

Mixed Numbers and Improper Fractions

Mixed numbers are made up of a whole number <u>AND</u> a fraction. It shows more than one whole thing.
Ex:

$1\frac{3}{4}$

                          1        $\frac{3}{4}$

All mixed numbers can be written as an <u>improper fraction</u> (remember, an improper fraction has a larger numerator than the denominator).

To change a mixed number into an improper fraction, you must multiply the whole number by the denominator, than add the numerator to get the new numerator. The denominator stays the same.

Ex:

$1\frac{3}{4} = \frac{7}{4}$

$(1 \times 4) + 3 = 7$, seven becomes the new numerator. Four stays as the denominator. Now the numerator is greater than the denominator

To change an improper fraction to a mixed number, you divide the denominator into the numerator.
Ex:

$$\frac{7}{5} = 1\frac{2}{5} \qquad 5\overline{)7} \\ \underline{-5} \\ \ \ 2$$

As you can see the 1 in the quotient is the whole number. The remainder 2 becomes the numerator and the <u>denominator</u> stays the <u>same</u>.
Ex:

$$\frac{19}{5} = 3\frac{4}{5} \qquad 5\overline{)19} \\ \underline{-15} \\ \ \ 4$$

* <u>Note</u> - When adding fractions, if you get an improper fraction for an answer, it <u>MUST</u> be changed into a mixed number.

If you get an improper fraction such as $\frac{6}{3}$, your answer will just be a whole number, no fraction.

$$\frac{6}{3} = 2$$

You will <u>NOT</u> have a zero for a numerator.

More examples for changing a mixed number into an improper fraction:

Ex:

$2\dfrac{1}{2} = \dfrac{5}{2}$ ← $(2 \times 2) + 1 = 5$

$4\dfrac{3}{5} = \dfrac{23}{5}$ ← $(4 \times 5) + 3 = 23$

$3\dfrac{1}{5} = \dfrac{16}{5}$ ← $(3 \times 5) + 1 = 16$

$3\dfrac{4}{5} = \dfrac{19}{5}$ ← $(3 \times 5) + 4 = 19$

$2\dfrac{3}{4} = \dfrac{11}{4}$ ← $(2 \times 4) + 3 = 11$

Examples of adding fractions and getting an improper fraction for an answer that must get changed to a mixed number.

Ex:

$\dfrac{3}{8} = \dfrac{3}{8}$

$\dfrac{3^{\times 2}}{4_{\times 2}} = \dfrac{6}{8}$

$+\ \dfrac{1^{\times 4}}{2_{\times 4}} = \dfrac{4}{8}$

$\dfrac{13}{8} = 1\dfrac{5}{8}$

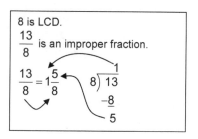

8 is LCD.

$\dfrac{13}{8}$ is an improper fraction.

$\dfrac{13}{8} = 1\dfrac{5}{8}$ $8\overline{)13}$
                                    $\underline{-8}$
                                      5

Ex:

$$\frac{7}{12}$$
$$\frac{9}{12}$$
$$+\frac{4}{12}$$
$$\frac{20}{12}=1\frac{8^{\div 4}}{12_{\div 4}}=1\frac{2}{3}$$

> Denominators are all the same, just add the numerators
>
> $\frac{20}{12}$ is an improper fraction
>
> $$\frac{20}{12}=1\frac{8}{12} \qquad 12\overline{)\begin{array}{r}1\\20\\-12\\\hline 8\end{array}}$$
>
> $1\frac{8}{12}$ must be put in simplest form to make $1\frac{2}{3}$

Comparing Mixed Numbers

When you compare mixed numbers, <u>FIRST</u> look at the whole numbers. If they are all <u>different</u>, just compare the whole numbers. You do not have to even look at the fraction parts.
Ex:

$$3\frac{2}{3} > 1\frac{4}{8}$$

3 is greater than

If the whole numbers are the <u>SAME</u>, you must compare the fractions. Simply use the short cut (cross multiplication) to compare.
Ex:

$$\overset{16}{3\frac{2}{3}} > \overset{12}{3\frac{4}{8}}$$

$2 \times 8 = 16$
$3 \times 4 = 12$
16 is greater than 12

$$\overset{15}{2\frac{3}{8}} > \overset{32}{2\frac{4}{5}}$$

$3 \times 5 = 15$
$8 \times 4 = 32$
15 is less than 32

117

Ordering Mixed Numbers

* Note - Be careful to follow the directions for ordering least to greatest or greatest to least.

If all of the whole numbers are different, simply order by whole numbers.

Least to Greatest

Ex:
$$3\frac{2}{3}, \ 1\frac{4}{5}, \ 6\frac{5}{8}, \ 2\frac{3}{7}, \ 9\frac{1}{3}$$

Answer:
$$1\frac{4}{5}, \ 2\frac{3}{7}, \ 3\frac{2}{3}, \ 6\frac{5}{8}, \ 9\frac{1}{3}$$

When the whole numbers are the same, you must make equivalent fractions so they all have the same denominator. The whole number won't change. Then match up with the original mixed numbers.

Ex:
$$2\frac{2}{3}^{\times 8}_{\times 8}, \ 2\frac{3}{6}^{\times 4}_{\times 4}, \ 2\frac{4}{12}^{\times 2}_{\times 2}, \ 2\frac{4}{24}$$

$$2\frac{16}{24}, \ 2\frac{12}{24}, \ 2\frac{8}{24}, \ 2\frac{4}{24}$$

④ ③ ② ①

24 is the LCD

Match and order L to G original group.

Answer: ⟶ $2\frac{4}{24}, \ 2\frac{4}{12}, \ 2\frac{3}{6}, \ 2\frac{2}{3}$

Order G to L

Ex:

$$4\frac{3}{4}, \ 2\frac{2}{3}, \ 4\frac{3}{8}, \ 1\frac{4}{6}$$

In this group, we have different whole numbers as well as two whole numbers that are the same.

First, compare the two that have the same whole numbers.

$$4\frac{3}{4} \overset{24}{>} 4\frac{3}{8}\overset{12}{}$$

$4\frac{3}{4}$ is the greatest.

Next, compare others by whole numbers.

$1\frac{4}{6}$ is the least for the whole group so that will go last.

Answer:

$$4\frac{3}{4}, \ 4\frac{3}{8}, \ 2\frac{2}{3}, \ 1\frac{4}{6}$$

If a group includes regular fractions, mixed numbers and improper fractions, you can do it different ways.

First, you can change improper fractions to mixed numbers or change the mixed numbers to improper fractions.

Changing all to improper fractions
L to G

Ex:

$$2\frac{1}{2},\ \frac{9}{4},\ \frac{8}{3},\ 1\frac{4}{5}$$

| LCD = 60 |

$$\frac{5^{\times 30}}{2_{\times 30}},\ \frac{9^{\times 15}}{4_{\times 15}},\ \frac{8^{\times 20}}{3_{\times 20}},\ \frac{9^{\times 12}}{5_{\times 12}}$$

$$\frac{150}{60},\ \frac{135}{60},\ \frac{160}{60},\ \frac{108}{60}$$

③ ② ④ ①

Answer:

$$1\frac{4}{5},\ \frac{9}{4},\ 2\frac{1}{2},\ \frac{8}{3}$$

| Match with original and put in order. |

Changing all to mixed numbers
Least to greatest

$$2\frac{1}{2},\ \frac{9}{4},\ \frac{8}{3},\ 1\frac{4}{5}$$

$$2\frac{1^{\times 6}}{2_{\times 6}},\ 2\frac{1^{\times 3}}{4_{\times 3}},\ 2\frac{2^{\times 4}}{3_{\times 4}},\ 1\frac{4}{5}$$

| 12 is the LCD |
| Match and order L to G original group. |

$$2\frac{6}{12},\ 2\frac{3}{12},\ 2\frac{8}{12},\ 1\frac{4}{5}$$

③ ② ④ ①

| * <u>Note</u> - $1\frac{4}{5}$ is the least, all others have a 2 as the whole number. So we only have to find the LCD for the others. |

Answer: → $1\frac{4}{5},\ \frac{9}{4},\ 2\frac{1}{2},\ \frac{8}{3}$

Estimating Fractions and Mixed Numbers to 0, $\frac{1}{2}$, 1

When estimating fractions, you must decide if a fraction is less than or more than $\frac{1}{2}$, closest to which whole number. It can also be rounded to $\frac{1}{2}$. To do this, look at the denominator and divide that number by 2.

Ex:

$\frac{3}{4} \approx 1$

$4 \div 2 = 2$ so $\frac{2}{4} = \frac{1}{2}$
$\frac{2}{4}$ is the <u>half</u> way point. 3 is greater than 2 so $\frac{3}{4}$ is closer to 1.

$\frac{1}{4} \approx 0$

Less than $\frac{1}{2}$, closer to 0

Ex:

$\frac{2}{6}$

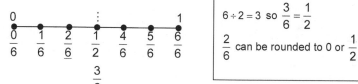

$6 \div 2 = 3$ so $\frac{3}{6} = \frac{1}{2}$
$\frac{2}{6}$ can be rounded to 0 or $\frac{1}{2}$

Ex:

$\frac{5}{8}$

$8 \div 2 = 4$ so $\frac{4}{8} = \frac{1}{2}$
$\frac{5}{8}$ is closest to $\frac{1}{2}$

Ex:

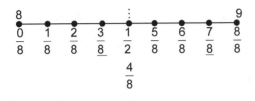

$8\frac{3}{8} \approx 8\frac{1}{2}$

$\frac{3}{8}$ is less than $\frac{1}{2}$ but it is closer to $\frac{1}{2}$ than to 8.

$8\frac{7}{8} \approx 9$

$\frac{7}{8}$ is greater than $\frac{1}{2}$ and closest to 9.

Adding and Subtracting Mixed Numbers

When adding and subtracting mixed numbers that have the <u>SAME</u> denominators, simply add or subtract whole numbers <u>AND</u> numerators. The denominator stays the same. Be sure to reduce the fraction to the lowest terms if necessary.
Ex:

$$4\frac{3}{9}$$
$$2\frac{2}{9}$$
$$+\phantom{2\frac{2}{9}}$$
$$6\frac{5}{9}$$

$$5\frac{8}{10}$$
$$2\frac{2}{10}$$
$$-\phantom{2\frac{2}{10}}$$
$$3\frac{6}{10} = 3\frac{3}{5}$$

$$\frac{6 \div 2}{10 \div 2} = \frac{3}{5}$$

* <u>Note</u> – If you have to put in simplest form, <u>first</u> bring over the whole number, and then change fraction to simplest form.

Ex:

$$1\frac{3}{9}$$
$$2\frac{7}{9}$$
$$+\phantom{2\frac{7}{9}}$$
$$3\frac{10}{9} = 3 + 1\frac{1}{9} = 4\frac{1}{9}$$

> If you get an improper fraction, it MUST be changed to a mixed number and then add the whole number for your final answer.

As you can see, $\frac{10}{9}$ changes to $1\frac{1}{9}$ then you add $3 + 1 = 4$.

$4\frac{1}{9}$ is the final answer.

When the mixed numbers have different denominators, you MUST find the LCD and make new equivalent fractions so that you can add or subtract. Whole numbers are brought over.

Ex:

$$3\frac{1^{\times 4}}{2_{\times 4}} = 3\frac{4}{8}$$

$$+\ 2\frac{1}{8} = 2\frac{1}{8}$$

$$\overline{\qquad\qquad 5\frac{5}{8}}$$

8 is the LCD

$\frac{1}{8}$ stays the same, just bring it over **AFTER** you bring the whole numbers over.

$\frac{1}{2}$ becomes $\frac{4}{8}$

* Note – Nothing goes under original parts.

Ex:

$$7\frac{1^{\times 6}}{4_{\times 6}} = 7\frac{6}{24}$$

$$6\frac{7^{\times 3}}{8_{\times 3}} = 6\frac{21}{24}$$

$$+\ 5\frac{1^{\times 8}}{3_{\times 8}} = 5\frac{8}{24}$$

$$\overline{\qquad\qquad 18\frac{35}{24}} = 18 + 1\frac{11}{24} = 19\frac{11}{24}$$

24 is the LCD

24 goes into 35 one time.
Subtract 24 from 35 to get 11.
So 11 is the new numerator.

Improper fraction becomes $1\frac{11}{24}$

* Note – When changing an improper fraction to a mixed number, if the whole number is 1, simply subtract the denominator from the numerator to get the new numerator.

$$\frac{35}{24} = 1\frac{11}{24}$$

24 goes into 35 one time
Subtract 24 from 35 to get 11
So 11 is the new numerator

Ex:

$$7\frac{4^{\times 4}}{5_{\times 4}} = 7\frac{16}{20}$$

$$-\ 2\frac{1^{\times 5}}{4_{\times 5}} = 2\frac{5}{20}$$

$$5\frac{11}{20}$$

20 is the LCD

When you subtract a mixed number from a whole number, you <u>MUST</u> <u>FIRST</u> change the whole number to a mixed number. To do this, look at the denominator on the given mixed number's fraction. You know that 1 whole equals a fraction that has the same number in the numerator <u>AND</u> denominator.

Ex:

$$\frac{4}{4} = 1$$

You have to borrow 1 whole from the whole number and change that 1 to a fraction so you can subtract.

Ex:

$$\cancel{8} = 7\frac{4}{4}$$

$$-\ 7\frac{3}{4} = 7\frac{3}{4}$$

$$\frac{1}{4}$$

You can <u>NOT</u> subtract $\frac{3}{4}$ from nothing so you borrow 1 whole from 8 = 7, the 1 changes to $\frac{4}{4}$ because you have a 4 as a denominator in $\frac{3}{4}$. Now you have two fractions to subtract

* <u>Note</u> – Nothing goes under the original group.

Ex.

$$\cancel{5} = 4\frac{8}{8}$$
$$-2\frac{5}{8} = 2\frac{5}{8}$$
$$\overline{\phantom{-2\frac{5}{8}}2\frac{3}{8}}$$

> Borrow 1 whole from 5 = 4. The 1 becomes $\frac{8}{8}$ because there is an 8 in $\frac{5}{8}$.

Ex:

$$5\frac{5}{8}$$
$$-1\phantom{\frac{5}{8}}$$
$$\overline{4\frac{5}{8}}$$

> Since the mixed number is on top, simply subtract the whole numbers and just bring down the fraction.

When you have two mixed numbers to subtract with different denominators, and after you have changed to equivalent fractions but still can't subtract because the top fraction is too small, you MUST borrow from the whole number to make a larger fraction, then you can subtract.

Ex:

$$4\frac{2^{\times 4}}{5_{\times 4}} = \cancel{4}\frac{8}{20} = 3\frac{28}{20}$$

$$-1\frac{3^{\times 5}}{4_{\times 5}} = 1\frac{15}{20} = 1\frac{15}{20}$$

$$2\frac{13}{20}$$

Cannot subtract

1. 20 is LCD
2. Bring whole numbers over
3. Make new fractions
4. Borrow 1 from 4 to make 3
5. 1 becomes $\frac{20}{20}$
6. Add $\frac{8}{20} + \frac{20}{20} = \frac{28}{20}$
7. Now you can subtract new mixed numbers

* <u>Note</u> – To get the new numerator of 28 simply add the old numerator and denominator so that $\frac{8}{20}$ is $8 + 20 = 28$.

Ex:

$$4\frac{1^{\times 3}}{4_{\times 3}} = \cancel{4}\frac{3}{12} = 3\frac{15}{12}$$

$$-3\frac{2^{\times 4}}{3_{\times 4}} = 3\frac{8}{12} = 3\frac{8}{12}$$

$$\frac{7}{12}$$

Can NOT subtract

12 is LCD

Ex:

$$8\frac{2^{\times 3}}{6_{\times 3}} = \cancel{8}\frac{\overset{18+}{6}}{18} = 7\frac{24}{18}$$

$$-\quad 3\frac{4^{\times 2}}{9_{\times 2}} = 3\frac{8}{18} = 3\frac{8}{18}$$

| 18 is LCD |

$$4\frac{16}{18} = 4\frac{8}{9}$$

↑ Can NOT subtract

Final answer is $4\frac{8}{9}$ after $\frac{16}{18}$ is put in simplest form.

Multiplying Fractions

Multiplying fractions is much easier than adding and subtracting fractions. Simply multiply the numerators then multiply the denominator. Simplify if needed.

Ex:
$$\frac{3}{5} \times \frac{2}{3} = \frac{6^{\div 3}}{15_{\div 3}} = \frac{2}{5}$$

Ex:
$$\frac{2}{3} \times \frac{5}{8} = \frac{10^{\div 2}}{24_{\div 2}} = \frac{5}{12}$$

Ex:
$$\frac{3}{8} \times \frac{4}{9} = \frac{12^{\div 12}}{72_{\div 12}} = \frac{1}{6}$$

If you can't think of the largest number that will go into larger numbers like 12 and 72, you can do it in more steps. Both are even numbers so each are divided by 2, also using your Rules of Divisibility, you know each number is divisible by 3, therefore also divisible by 6.

OR

$$\frac{3}{8} \times \frac{4}{9} = \frac{12^{\div 2}}{72_{\div 2}} = \frac{6^{\div 6}}{36_{\div 6}} = \frac{1}{6}$$

OR

$$\frac{3}{8} \times \frac{4}{9} = \frac{12^{\div 3}}{72_{\div 3}} = \frac{4^{\div 4}}{24_{\div 4}} = \frac{1}{6}$$

OR

$$\frac{3}{8} \times \frac{4}{9} = \frac{12^{\div 6}}{72_{\div 6}} = \frac{2^{\div 2}}{12_{\div 2}} = \frac{1}{6}$$

<u>All</u> have a final answer $\frac{1}{6}$

Short Cut for Multiplying Fractions

Sometimes you can use the short cut to automatically getting the simplest form of the answer the first time that you multiply. To do this, you cross divide diagonally by the <u>SAME</u> number. This makes the original numbers smaller.

Ex:

$$\frac{\cancel{3}^{\div 3 \,\, 1}}{5} \times \frac{2}{\cancel{3}_{\div 3 \,\, 1}} = \frac{2}{5}$$

Diagonally 3 can go into both 3's to make them each 1, then:
$1 \times 2 = 2 \qquad 5 \times 1 = 5$

Long way

$$\frac{3}{5} \times \frac{2}{3} = \frac{6^{\div 3}}{15_{\div 3}} = \frac{2}{5}$$

Same answers

Ex:

$$\frac{\cancel{2}^{\div 2 \,\, 1}}{3} \times \frac{5}{\cancel{8}_{\div 2 \,\, 4}} = \frac{5}{12}$$

$1 \times 5 = 5$
$3 \times 4 = 12$

Ex:

$$\frac{\cancel{3}^{\div 3 \,\, 1}}{\cancel{8}_{\div 4 \,\, 2}} \times \frac{\cancel{4}^{\div 4 \,\, 1}}{\cancel{9}_{\div 3 \,\, 3}} = \frac{1}{6}$$

$1 \times 1 = 1$
$2 \times 3 = 6$

Multiplying Mixed Numbers

First, you need to change the mixed numbers into improper fractions. Do cross dividing if possible, then multiply and last, put final answer into a mixed number.

Ex:

$$2\frac{2}{8} \times 4\frac{4}{9}$$

$$\frac{\cancel{18}^{\div 9 \, 2}}{\cancel{8}_{\div 8 \, 1}} \times \frac{\cancel{40}^{\div 8 \, 5}}{\cancel{9}_{\div 9 \, 1}} = \frac{10}{1} = 10$$

1. Change to improper fractions
2. Cross divide diagonally
3. Multiply $2 \times 5 = 10$
   $1 \times 1 = 1$
   $\frac{10}{1} = 10$

Ex:

$$1\frac{3}{4} \times 2\frac{3}{5}$$

$$\frac{7}{4} \times \frac{13}{5} = \frac{91}{20} = 4\frac{11}{20}$$

1. Change to improper fractions
2. Can NOT cross divide
3. Multiply as is
4. Change improper fraction to a mixed number

Final answer = $4\frac{11}{20}$

Dividing Fractions

To divide by a fraction, you use the **reciprocal** which means you flip the second fraction and change the division sign to a times sign to multiply. Simplify if needed.

Ex:
$$\frac{4}{9} \div \frac{3}{5} = \frac{4}{9} \times \frac{5}{3} = \frac{20}{27}$$

1. Changed ÷ to ×
2. Reciprocal of $\frac{3}{5}$ is $\frac{5}{3}$
3. Multiply

Ex:
$$2 \div \frac{1}{7} = \frac{2}{1} \times \frac{7}{1} = \frac{14}{1} = 14$$

* <u>Note</u> – Remember, every whole number has a one for a denominator.

Ex:
$$3\frac{3}{4} \div \frac{1}{4} = \frac{15}{4} \times \frac{4}{1} = \frac{60}{4} = \frac{15}{1} = 15$$

Proof!

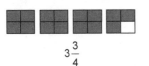

$3\frac{3}{4}$

Each whole is divided into 4 parts. When you count all of the shaded parts, there are 15 parts

Chapter 7:

GRAPHS

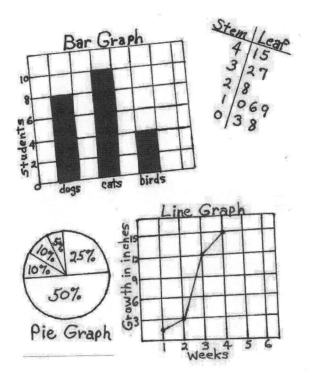

Range, Median, Mode, and Mean

Range – the range of a group of numbers is the difference (-) between the least and the greatest number.

Median – the median is the middle number of a group of numbers. (median of a highway separates opposing lanes)

Mode – the mode is the number that is repeated the <u>most</u> in a group of numbers. If no number is repeated, then there is <u>no</u> mode.

* <u>Note</u> – you can't use a zero

Mean – the mean of a group of numbers is the average of the numbers. To figure an average, you first add all the numbers then divide by the amount of numbers that you added.

When you are asked to do any or all of the above for a group of numbers, the <u>FIRST</u> step that you <u>MUST</u> do is put all of the numbers in <u>ORDER</u>.

Example: A set of grades on tests:

         100 85 60 100 92 95 73

         Step 1 – Put in order from least to greatest

         60 73 85 92 95 100 100

* <u>Note</u> – double check to be sure you have <u>all</u> the numbers. There are seven in this group)

60 73 85 92 95 100 100

<u>Range</u> – the difference between 100 and 60.

$$100 - 60 = 40 \qquad Range = 40$$

<u>Median</u> – the middle number. (If there is an odd amount of numbers, the center number is the media.)

Median = 92

(One way to <u>find</u> the median is to cross out opposite ends until you get to the center.
~~60~~ ~~73~~ ~~85~~ (92) ~~95~~ ~~100~~ ~~100~~)

If there is an even amount of numbers, you may have to find the numbers that would be in the center.

Ex: ~~60~~ ~~73~~ 85 | 92 ~~95~~ ~~100~~

Median = 88.5

| 86 87 88 89 90 91 |
| 88.5 is in the middle between 85 & 92) |
| Find the mean for 85 and 92 |

<u>Mode</u> - the number used the <u>most</u>.

Mode =100   (there are two 100's and only one of each other number)

<u>Mean</u> – the average of the numbers

	Step 1 – Add	Step 2 – Divide by 7
	100	86.42
	100	7) 605.00
	95	<u>−56</u>
	92	45
	85	<u>−42</u>
	73	30
	<u>+60</u>	<u>−28</u>
Mean = 86.42	605	20
Average Grade = 86		<u>−14</u>
		6

135

Ex: 8 12 10 2 6 4 – original numbers

      2 4 6 | 8 10 12 - in order

Range - 12 – 2 = 10

Median - 7   (between 6 & 8)

Mode -   No mode (no numbers are repeated)

Mean -   7

2 + 4 + 6 + 8 + 10 + 12 = 42

$$6 \overline{)42} = 7$$
$$\underline{-42}$$
$$0$$

Ex: 64 58 61 59 58 – original numbers

       58 58 59 61 64 - in order

Range - 64 – 58 = 6

Median - 59

Mode -   58

Mean -   60

58 + 58 + 59 + 61 + 64 = 300

Mean Steps:

$$5 \overline{)300} = 60$$
$$\underline{-30}$$
$$0$$

Ex: 1098   749   751   843   998   943 – original numbers

　　　　749   751   843₊₅₀   ₋₅₀943   998   1098 – in order

Range - 1098 – 749 = 349

Median - 893 (943 – 843 = 100 ÷ 2 = 50)
　　　　　　　(843 + 50 = 893)

Mode - No mode (no numbers are repeated)

Mean - 897

749 + 751 + 843 + 943 + 998 + 1098 = 5382

Mean Steps:

```
      897
   6) 5382
     −48
      58
     −54
      42
     −42
       0
```

Reading and Making Graphs

Graphs are different ways of showing information.

Types of graphs include pictographs, bar graphs, line graphs, pie (circle) graphs, line plots, stem-and-leap, and coordinate graphs (such as on maps).

Every graph has a title pertaining to the topic or information that the graph is about.

Some graphs may have a key or legend to show certain information such as what a symbol means or on a map to show distance.

Examples of different kinds of graphs:

Pictograph – has symbol to represent the amounts.

Ex:
Favorite Kinds of Stories in 4th Grade Class

Sports	😊😊😊◖	= 14 students
Mystery	😊😊	= 8 students
Animal	😊😊😊😊😊	= 20 students

Most students like animal stories.

Key: 😊 = 4 students

◖ = 2 students

Bar Graphs – these graphs can be set up horizontally (across) or vertically (up and down). In <u>all</u> bar graphs there **MUST** be a space bar separating the information bars.

Ex: **Horizontal Bar Graph**

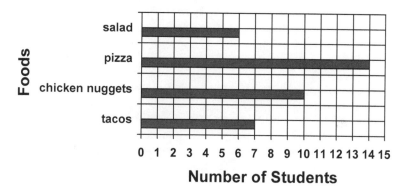

* <u>Note</u> – scale for numbers is counting by ones.

* <u>Note</u> – notice the space bars between shaded bars, <u>plus</u> space bar between tacos line and the bottom.

Pizza is the most popular lunch item in the cafeteria.

Ex: **Vertical Bar Graph**

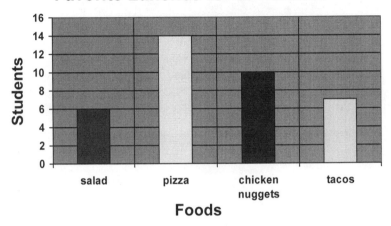

* Note – the spaces between bars and at each end.

* Note – scale for numbers is counting by two's.

Both bar graphs show the same information.

* Note – Horizontal bar graphs have the numbers (quantities) across the bottom and the item being compared on the left of the graph.

* Note – Vertical bar graphs have the quantities on the left side and the items on the bottom.

1. **Line Graphs** – line graphs are used to show changes <u>over time</u>.

Ex:

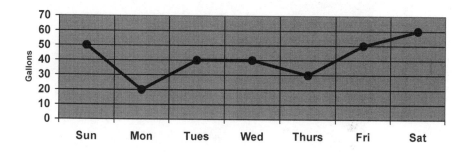

* <u>Note</u> – scale of numbers is counting by ten's

More gallons of ice cream are sold on Saturday and Sunday than any other days of the week.

* Times, days, etc.... go along the bottom

Ex:

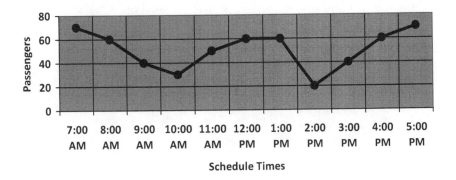

* Note – Scale for passengers is counting by 10's

This graph shows that the bus is fullest first time and last time of the bus's day with people going to and coming from work. Another busy time is lunch time.

Circle Graphs (Pie Graphs) – circle graphs show how parts are related to the whole using either fractions or percentages. The whole circle is 100%, so if you use percents, all of the percents must add up to 100 for 100%.

If you use fractions, all the fractions must add up to one 1 as a whole number.

Ex:

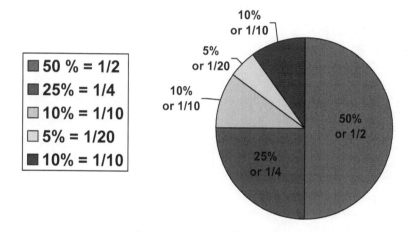

Most Popular Colors

- 50 % = 1/2
- 25% = 1/4
- 10% = 1/10
- 5% = 1/20
- 10% = 1/10

* Note – all percent numbers add up to 100%

Using Fractions

$50\% = \dfrac{1}{2}$ $\dfrac{1}{2} = \dfrac{10}{20}$

$25\% = \dfrac{1}{4}$ $\dfrac{1}{4} = \dfrac{5}{20}$

$5\% = \dfrac{1}{20}$ $\dfrac{2}{10} = \dfrac{4}{20}$

$10\% = \dfrac{1}{10}$ $+\dfrac{1}{20} = \dfrac{1}{20}$

$\dfrac{20}{20} = 1$ whole

Line Plots – line plots use *x*'s for counting how many items or units that are in each category.

Ex:

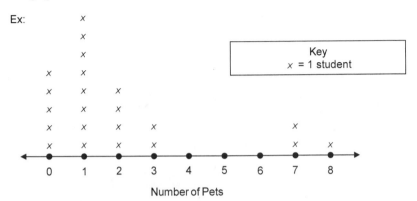

This line plot shows that 5 students have no pets, 8 students each have 1 pet, 4 students each have 2 pets, 2 students have 3 pets each, no students have 4 or 5 pets, 2 students each have 6 pets and 1 student has 8 pets.

Find the range, mode, and median for the number of pets.

Range = 8

Mode = 1 pet

Median = 11

$8 - 0 = 8$

Most students have 1 pet.
11 *x*'s (of 22 *x*'s) is the middle which is in the 1 pet group

Stem-and-Leaf Plots – Another way of showing information that also can easily be used to find range, median, mode, and mean is the stem-and-leaf plot.

Set up looks like this ⟶

Stem	Leaf
2	2 5 8
1	0 4 3 9
0	6 7

Stem side shows tens
Leaf side shows ones

Bottom row shows no tens (0), singles 6 and 7

Second row shows 1 ten PLUS 4, 3, 7 to mean 10, 14, 13, 19

Top row shows 2 tens (20) PLUS 2, 5, 8 to mean 22, 25, 28

When you are given a set of numbers and/or a stem-and-leaf plot such as the example above, and the numbers are **NOT** in order, you **MUST FIRST** put all the numbers in order before you can correctly find the range, etc....

Using the above example, you can see the middle row is NOT in order, so you MUST rewrite the whole stem-and-leaf in order.

Stem	Leaf
2	2̶ 5̶ 8̶
1	0̶ ③ 4̶ 9̶
0	6̶ 7̶

6 is the smallest number, 28 is the largest number

Range = 22

Median = 14

Mode = no mode

Mean = 16

```
  6          16
  7       9)144
 10         -9
 13          54
 14         -54
 19           0
 22
 25
+28
144
```

$28 - 6 = 22$

Center number – cross out opposites

No number is repeated

Figure average, +, ÷

* <u>Note</u> – this stem-and-leaf has the largest numbers on the top row, it can also be set up so the largest numbers are on the bottom row. Outcomes will be the same.

Stem	Leaf
0	6 7
1	0 3 4 9
2	2 5 8

Ex:

Directions: Put the following quiz grades in a stem-and-leaf plot.

100 89 94 85 76 93 93 89 75   (9 numbers)

First – put the numbers in order

75 76 85 89 89 93 93 94 100   (9 numbers)

* Note – double check to make sure you copied correctly and didn't leave any out.

Stem	Leaf
7	5̶ 6̶
8	5̶ 9̶ ⑨
9	3̶ 3̶ 4̶
100	0̶

9 numbers on leaf side

Find:

Range = 25 $100 - 75 = 25$

Median = 89   Center number.

Mode = 89 and 93   both are repeated twice

Mean = 88   + and ÷

```
       75
       76
       85
       89
       89
       93
       93
       94
     +100
      794
```

$$\begin{array}{r} 88.2 \\ 9\overline{)794.0} \\ \underline{-72} \\ 74 \\ \underline{-72} \\ 20 \\ \underline{-18} \\ 2 \end{array}$$

88.2 rounded to the nearest whole number is 88.

Double Line Graph - a line graph can show two different comparisons over the same time frame.

Ex:

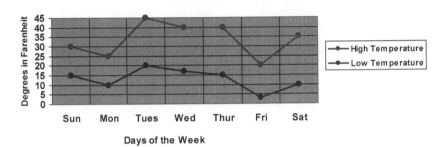

Average High = 33.6°F

Sun	30
Mon	25
Tues	45
Wed	40
Thurs	40
Fri	20
Sat	+35
	235

```
      33.57
7) 235.00
   -21
    25
   -21
    40
   -35
    50
   -49
     1
```

Average Low = 12.6°F

Sun	15
Mon	8
Tues	20
Wed	17
Thurs	15
Fri	3
Sat	+10
	88

```
      12.57
7) 88.00
   -7
   18
  -14
   40
  -35
   50
  -49
    1
```

Double Bar Graph - A double bar graph can be used to compare two events or groups.

Ex:

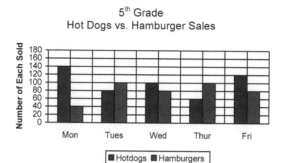

Some 5th Graders bring their lunch, buy pizza, or salads.

Hot dogs are more popular than hamburgers.

* <u>Note</u> – space bar at beginning and the end <u>and</u> between the <u>days</u>.

Chapter 8:

Measurements

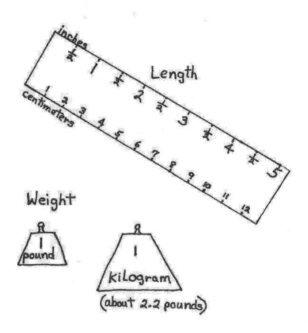

Measurements

There are two systems for all measurements, the **U.S. Customary Standard System** and the **Metric System**. The majority of the world uses the metric system.

We will start each section with U.S. customary standard units and then show how the metric units work.

Linear Measurement – Length

U.S. Standard Units (Basic Units)

12 inches	=	1 foot	(standard ruler)
3 feet	=	1 yard	(yard stick) = 36 inches
5280 feet	=	1 mile	
1760 yards	=	1 mile	

One inch can be divided into fractional parts.

1 inch (actual size) =

1 inch enlarged to show parts:

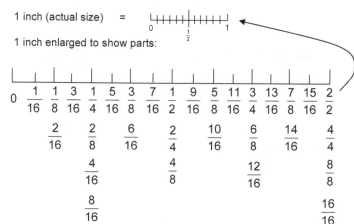

All of the parts are in one inch

Look very carefully at a ruler on the inches side and you will see all of the parts within each inch.

These tiny parts are extremely important for all carpentry work, in construction of all buildings, bridges, any metal work, the Space Shuttle, cars, ships, etc. Everything that is constructed in anyway must have the correct, precise measurements so that all parts fit perfectly.

In a house, if the carpenters do not measure everything correctly, the windows and doors would not fit properly, walls would not be straight, the roof would leak, and eventually the house would fall down.

First and foremost, the foundation has to be perfect or the rest of the house would not work right.

Enlarged Parts of an Inch

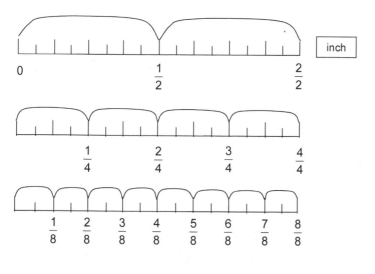

As you can see, equivalent fractions are under each other.

$$\frac{1}{2}=\frac{2}{4}=\frac{8}{16} \qquad \frac{1}{4}=\frac{2}{8}=\frac{4}{16} \qquad \frac{3}{4}=\frac{6}{8}=\frac{12}{16} \qquad \frac{2}{2}=\frac{4}{4}=\frac{8}{8}=\frac{16}{16}$$

Converting Linear Measurements

When changing one unit of measurement to another, you must think of the units that make up the basic measurements. If you are asked how many inches are in a number of feet, first ask yourself how many inches make up 1 foot, and then multiply that by the number of feet to get the total number of inches.

Ex:

     L   s   (Basic Units)
  6 ft = 72 in   12 in = 1 ft, so multiply
                           6 × 12 = 72

(Basic Units are 12 inches = 1 foot. So 12 in times 6 ft = 72 in)

* Rule - L (large unit) to s (small unit) you multiply L to S ×

When going from large units (feet) to small units (inches) multiply by the basis unit times 12 because there are 12 inches in 1 foot.

Ex:

     L   s   (Basic Units)
  5 miles = 26,400 ft   5280 ft = 1 mi, so multiply
                           5280 × 5 = 26,400 ft

(Basic Units are 5280 feet = 1 mile. So 5280 ft times 5 mi = 26,400 ft)

* Note – I had my student put this rule at the top of their paper AND over the units, as you see above.

Rule -   s to L ÷

When going from small units to large units, use the rule s to L ÷. Use the basic units to divide.

Ex:
$$\begin{array}{cc} s & ?\ L \\ 180\ in & =\ \underline{15}\ ft \end{array}$$

(Inches are a smaller unit than feet. 12 inches equals 1 foot, so divide by 12)

$$180 \div 12 = 15$$

These two rules work on all kinds of measurements including metrics.

Ex:

| L | s | | (Basic Units) |
| 14 yds | = $\underline{42}$ ft | | × 3 (3 ft = 1 yd) |

| L | | s |
| 11 ft, 8 in | = | $\underline{140}$ in | × 12 + 8 (12 in = 1 ft)

| s | L |
| 42 in | = $\underline{3}$ ft, $\underline{6}$ in | ÷ 12, and remainder of 6 in

| s | L |
| 29 ft | = $\underline{9}$ yds, $\underline{2}$ ft | ÷ 3 (3 ft = 1 yd) and remainder of ft

* <u>Note</u> – when dividing, if you get a remainder, it will always be in the smaller units.

Adding and Multiplying Linear Measurements

When you add or multiply linear measurements, you often need to convert (change) your answer to show the greatest units.

Ex:

```
   4yds 2ft
  +1yd  1ft
  ─────────
   5yds 3ft = 6yds
         ↓
        1yd
```

> * Note – <u>FIRST</u> bring down unit labels, then add each part.

Now look at the smaller unit to see if it can change to the larger unit. Yes, because 3 feet = 1 yard so 1 yard gets added to 5 yards to equal 6 yards as your final answer.

Ex:

```
    9ft  9in
  + 3ft  5in
  ──────────
   12ft 14in
```

> * Note – <u>FIRST</u> bring down unit labels, then add each group separately. DO <u>NOT</u> carry 1 of 14 over into the feet part.

(14)
Now look at the inches, since 12 inches equals 1 foot, you can take 12 from 14 and make 1 foot with 2 inches left over. Add 1 foot to 12 feet to get 13 feet and <u>2 inches.</u>

Now ask if anything can be changed with the feet. Yes!
3 ft = 1 yd so 13 ft = 12 ft making <u>4 yds</u> with <u>1 ft</u> left.

So the <u>final</u> answer is 4 yds 1 ft 2 in

Ex:

$4 \times$ 2ft 7in

```
  2ft  7in
×        4
─────────
  8ft 28in
```

*Note – FIRST bring down unit labels, then multiply each group separately. DO NOT carry the 2 of 28 over into the feet side.

Now convert inches to feet

```
 8ft  28in
   − 24   = 2ft
      4in
```
10ft 4in

Now convert feet to yards

```
10ft  4in
 − 9      = 3yds
  1ft  4in
```

So final answer is <u>3 yds 1 ft 4 in</u>

Ex:

```
   4yds 9in
×         7
───────────
  28yds 63in
     −36  = 1yd
     +27in
     −24  = 2ft
        3
```

Change 63 in to 1yd 27in
+28yds
───────────
29yds 27in

Change 27 in to 2ft 3in

Final answer = 29 yds 2 ft 3 in

Ex:

        L   s   (Basic Units)
4 miles = <u>21,120</u> ft   (5280 ft = 1 mi)

       L   s
3 miles = <u>5280</u> yds   (1760 yds = 1 mi)

       L   s
38 yards = <u>114</u> feet   (3 ft = 1 yd)

* <u>Note</u> – remember rule L to s ×

Ex:

    s   L
62 in = 5 ft 2 in   (÷ 12)
   s   L
420 ft = 140 yds   (÷ 3)

      s   L
18,960 yds = 10 mi 1360 yds   (÷ 1760 yds = 1 mi)

* <u>Note</u> – remember the rules

    L to s   × by basic units

    s to L   ÷ by basic units

Metric System

Most of the countries of the world use the metric system for all measurements. The metric system is a base 10 system; 10's, 100's, 1000's.

Linear Measurements

Metric units of length are made up of millimeters (smallest units), centimeters, decimeters, meters, and kilometers.

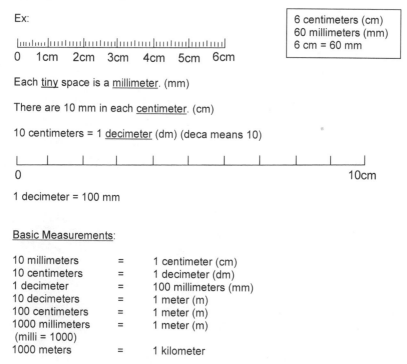

Ex:

6 centimeters (cm)
60 millimeters (mm)
6 cm = 60 mm

Each <u>tiny</u> space is a <u>millimeter</u>. (mm)

There are 10 mm in each <u>centimeter</u>. (cm)

10 centimeters = 1 <u>decimeter</u> (dm) (deca means 10)

1 decimeter = 100 mm

Basic Measurements:

10 millimeters	=	1 centimeter (cm)
10 centimeters	=	1 decimeter (dm)
1 decimeter	=	100 millimeters (mm)
10 decimeters	=	1 meter (m)
100 centimeters	=	1 meter (m)
1000 millimeters (milli = 1000)	=	1 meter (m)
1000 meters	=	1 kilometer

(A meter stick is about 3 inches longer than a yard stick which is 36 inches long, so a meter stick is about 39 inches long.)

The width of a regular paperclip is 1 cm wide. The thickness of one side is 1 mm.

Long distances are measured in kilometers. 1000 meters equals 1 kilometer.

A mile equals 1760 yards. Remember, a meter is about 3 inches longer than a yard so thinking in yards, it takes more kilometers to equal the same distance as miles.

1 mile equals 1.6 kilometers.

Look at the speedometer in your car to compare how many kilometers equal the same distance in miles.

30 mi	≈	50 km
50 mi	≈	80 km
60 mi	≈	100 km
96 mi	≈	160 km

Basic Metric Linear Units

1 cm	=	10 mm
1 dm	=	10 cm or 100 mm
1 m	=	10 dm or 100 cm or 1000 mm
1 km	=	1000 meters

Then:

6 cm	=	60 mm	(just x, 6 x 10)
4 dm	=	40 cm	(just x, 4 x 10)
3 m	=	30 dm	(just x, 3 x 10)
3 m	=	300 cm	(just x, 3 x 100)
3 m	=	3000 mm	(just x, 3 x 1000)

Always put your basic units at the top of your paper when you have to figure how many units are in each group.

Then use the following rules when going from one set of units to another.

L to s, ×

s to L, ÷   (Look familiar?)

Put rules at the top of your work page AND on top of your labels.

Ex:

L		s	
8 cm	=	80 mm	× by 10
50 dm	=	5000 mm	× by 100
15 cm	=	150 mm	× by 10

s		L	
200 cm	=	20 dm	÷ by 10
8000 mm	=	8 m	÷ by 1000
400 mm	=	4 dm	÷ by 100

Centimeters, Meters, and Decimals

The same basic rules apply except you ONLY have to move the decimal point to the right or left.

Remember, every whole number has a decimal point on its right so 8 = 8.

When going from small to large, simply move the decimal point (.) to the LEFT one place if you are dividing by 10.

Ex:

      S   L
  62.3 mm = 6.23 cm

The decimal point (.) moved one place to the left because we divided by 10 since there are 10 mm in 1 cm. (One place to the left because there is only one zero in 10)

Proof!

```
          6.23
    10) 62.30
        -60
         23
        -20
         30
        -30
          0
```

If you are dividing by 100, move the decimal point (.) <u>two</u> places to the left.

Ex:

        S   L
   2461 cm   =   24.61 m

The decimal point (.) moved two places to the left (2461.) since there is a decimal point (.) on the right of the whole number and we divide by 100 because there are 100 centimeters in 1 meter.

* <u>Note</u> – just remember, move the decimal point (.) to match the number of zero's; 1 for 10, 2 for 100, 3 for 1000, etc…

When going from large to small units, move the decimal point (.) to the right according to the number of zeros in 1<u>0</u>, 1<u>00</u>, 1<u>000</u>, because you are multiplying.

Ex:

       L   S
   42.1 cm   =   421 mm

We moved the decimal point (.) <u>one</u> place to the <u>right</u> because we are multiplying by 1<u>0</u>.

* <u>Note</u> – remember if the answer becomes a whole number, we don't show the decimal point (.) on the far right of the number but it is really still there.

Ex:
        L   s
   0.54m = 54 cm

We moved the decimal point (.) two places to the right because we multiply by 1<u>00</u> (two places because there are two zero's in 1<u>00</u>)

   s to L • ⟵ ÷

   L to s • ⟶ ×

| This shows the direction the • must go |

Writing the following in cm and m:

	cm	m
5 m 70 cm =	570 cm	5.7 m
4 m 39 cm =	439 cm	4.39 m
8 m 19 cm =	819 cm	8.19 m
6 m 76 cm =	676 cm	6.76 m

Proof!   5 m 70 cm
           ↓   ↘
          500 cm + 70 cm = 570 cm

          5 m 70 cm
           ↓ ↙
          5.7 m

5 whole meters 70 cm out of 100 cm that make 1 meter

$$\frac{70}{100} = \frac{7}{10}$$

Activities for Linear Measurements

Whatever room you are in, choose ten objects that can be measured. These objects can include the length of a wall, door, window, area rug, table top, book, etc. You get the idea. On your paper make columns for comparison in inches, feet, yards, versus centimeters, decimeter, and meters.

Using a road map, compare long distances using miles versus kilometers.

U.S. Customary Weights

We measure weight by ounces, pounds, and tons.

Basic Units –

    1 pound (lb) = 16 ounces
    1 Ton = 2000 pounds

To convert from one unit to another, you are going to × or ÷ by the basic units listed above.

The same rules apply as before. If you are going from large units to small units, you will multiply. If you go from small units to large units, you will divide.

Ex:

    L   s
  3 lb = <u>48</u> oz.

| Multiply by 16 since 16 oz is the basic units for 1 pound |

Ex:

    L   s
  4 T = <u>8000</u> lb

| Multiply by 2000 since 2000 lb is the basic units for 1 ton |

Ex:

      L   s
  8 lb 9 oz = <u>137</u> oz.

| Multiply 8 × 16 (since 16 oz is the basic units for 1 pound) then add 9 |

Ex:

$$\begin{array}{cc} \text{s} & \text{L} \\ 10{,}000 \text{ lb} & = \underline{5} \text{ T} \end{array}$$

÷ by 2000 since 2000 is the basic unit for 1 Ton

Ex:

$$\begin{array}{cc} \text{s} & \text{L} \\ 92 \text{ oz} & = \underline{5 \text{ lb } 12 \text{ oz}} \end{array}$$

÷ by 16 since 16 is the basic unit for 1 pound, remainder becomes ounces left over

Ex:

$$\begin{array}{cc} \text{L} & \text{s} \\ 5 \text{ T } 832 \text{ lb} & = \underline{10{,}832 \text{ lb}} \end{array}$$

5 × 2000 + 832

U.S. Customary Measurements of Capacity

Capacity means how much an object can hold, whether it is a liquid or dry goods.

Dry goods = same as weight

    1 lb = 16 ounces (oz)
    1 T = 2000 pounds (lb)

Ex:

    5 lb bag of flour or sugar
    2 oz container of a spice

Now think of your mom's cooking and baking. She uses measuring spoons, cups, pints, quarts, and gallons for both liquid and dry measurements.

A recipe may call for 2 cups of flour and $\frac{1}{2}$ cup milk.

Measuring Basics

teaspoons and **tablespoons**

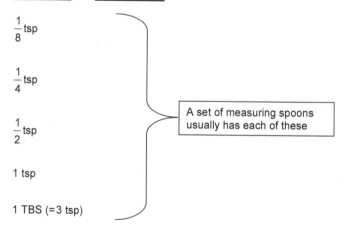

$\frac{1}{8}$ tsp

$\frac{1}{4}$ tsp

$\frac{1}{2}$ tsp

1 tsp

1 TBS (=3 tsp)

A set of measuring spoons usually has each of these

Cups

1 cup = 16 TBS = 8 oz

Set of measuring cups include: $\frac{1}{4}$ c, $\frac{1}{3}$ c, $\frac{1}{2}$ c, $\frac{2}{3}$ c, $\frac{3}{4}$ c, and 1 c

Gallons

Use Mr. Gallon Man to learn the different parts of a pint, quart, and gallon.

Mr. Gallon Man

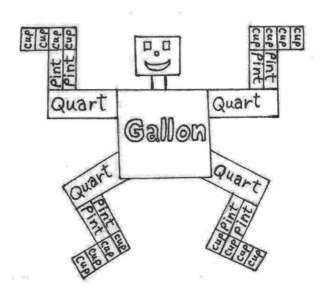

8 oz = 1 cup	4 quarts = 1 gallon	16 cups = 1 gallon
2 cups = 1 pint	4 cups = 1 quart	16 Tbs = 1 cup
2 pints = 1 quart	8 pints = 1 gallon	

Basic Measurements of Mr. Gallon Man

1 cup = 8 ounces = 16 tablespoons

1 pint = 2 cups

1 quart = 2 pints = 4 cups

1 gallon = 4 quarts = 8 pints = 16 cups = 128 ounces

$\frac{1}{2}$ gallon = 64 ounces (half a gallon of milk)

When working with liquids, you will see FL oz for fluid ounces.

When converting from one unit to another, think of the basic units that make up the two units and multiply if you are going from a large unit to a small unit or divide if you are going from a small unit to a large unit.

Ex:

   L s
 3 qt = ____ c

Think of how many cups make one quart (4)
4 × 3
So 3 quarts = <u>12 c</u>

Ex:
$$\overset{S}{20\text{ pt}} = \underline{} \overset{L}{\text{gal}}$$

Think of how many pints make one gallon (8 pints).
Divide 8 into 20, which equals 2 gallons with 4 pints left over.

$4\text{ pt} = \dfrac{1}{2}\text{ gal}$ so $20\text{ pt} = 2\dfrac{1}{2}\text{ gal}$

Ex:
$$\overset{S}{28\text{ FL oz}} = \underline{} \overset{L}{\text{pt}}$$

Think of how many ounces make one pint (16 ounces).
Divide 16 into 28, which equals 1 pint with 12 FL oz left over.

$\dfrac{12}{16}$ reduced to the lowest terms = $\dfrac{3}{4}$ so 28 FL oz = $1\dfrac{3}{4}$ pt

Ex:
$$\overset{L}{1\text{ pt 12 FL oz}} = \underline{} \overset{S}{\text{c}}$$

Think of how many cups are in one pint (2 cups).

Think of how many cups are in 12 FL oz (8 oz = 1 c so 12 FL oz = $1\dfrac{1}{2}$ c).

Divide 16 into 28, which equals 1 pint with 12 FL oz left over.

$1\text{ pt 12 FL oz} = 3\dfrac{1}{2}\text{ c}$

We added 2 c plus 1 c to get 3 cups.

Ex:
$$\overset{S}{18\text{ tsp}} = \underline{} \overset{L}{\text{TBS}}$$

Think of how many teaspoons make one tablespoon (3 teaspoons).
Divide 18 by 3 = 6

18 tsp = <u>6 TBS</u>

Metric Weight

Look at any can, box, bag, or package that you can have in the cupboard, pantry, and refrigerator. You will see the U.S. standard measurement in ounces (oz) and/or pounds (lbs), and the metric weight in milligrams, grams, and/or kilograms.

The smallest unit of weight in the metric system is a milligram (mg), the weight of a single regular paperclip. Next is a gram (g). It takes 1000 mg to equal 1 g. Then a kilogram (kg) equals 1000 grams (g), 1000 kilograms equal 1 metric ton.

Find several items in the cupboard, and/or refrigerator and compare the two systems of measurements. Include heavy items such as a can of coffee, bag of flour or sugar, a large can of beans, etc.

Ex:

Can of whole peeled tomatoes in thick puree

U.S.	Metric
28 oz (1 lb 12 oz)	794 g

Container of Folgers coffee

U.S.	Metric
34 oz (2 lbs 2 oz)	960 g

Ex:

Peanut Butter

<u>U.S</u>.   <u>Metric</u>

1 lb   452 g
(16 oz)   (0.452 kg)

Chili Powder

<u>U.S</u>.   <u>Metric</u>

1.5 oz   42 g

As you can see, the metric system deals in much larger numbers, but the basic units are based on 1000. So if you look at the jar of peanut butter that weighs one pound, which is the same as 454 g, then 1000 g which is 1 kilogram equals just less than two pounds. One pound is a little less than $\frac{1}{2}$ kilogram.

Converting from Grams to Kilograms

The same rules apply here as to centimeter and meters.

Put the rules at the top of your paper. 1 kg = 1000 g

L to s • ⟶ × 1000   s to L • ⟵ ÷ 1000

* <u>Note</u> – remember, the above arrow show what direction the decimal point moves when you either multiply or divide, AND it is going to move 3 places because there are 3 zeros in 1<u>000</u>.

Ex:
        L   s
   5.9 kg = <u>5900 g</u>

Multiply 1000, just move the decimal point (.) 3 places to the right.
5.900 = 5900

Ex:
        L   s
   0.32 kg = <u>320 g</u>

Multiply 1000, just move the decimal point (.) 3 places to the right.
0.320 = 320

Ex:
        s   L
   6 g = <u>0.006 kg</u>

Divide 1000, just move the decimal point (.) 3 places to the left.
0006. = 0.006

Ex:
        s   L
   1500 g = <u>1.5 kg</u>

Divide 1000, just move the decimal point (.) 3 places to the left.
1500. = 1.5

Ex:
        s   L
   63,481 g = 63.481 kg

Divide 1000, just move the decimal point (.) 3 places to the left.
63481. = 63.481

Metric Capacity

The smallest metric measurement for capacity is a milliliter (ml). To understand how small a milliliter is, think about a raindrop or drops in an eyedropper.

Basic Units

1000 milliliters (mL) = <u>1 liter</u> (L)

A liter is a little larger than a quart.

1 quart = 946 mL

If a liter equals 1000 mL, you can see that 1 quart is smaller than 1000 mL.

Look at the differences on a carton of milk, bottle of juice, or a large bottle of soda.

Basic Units

1000 liters (L) = 1 kiloliter (kl)
(about 1,056 quarts)

The same rules apply for converting from one unit to another unit.

Ex:
    L   s
  4 L = <u>4000 mL</u>

| Multiply by 1000 |

Ex:
    L   s
  0.7 L = <u>700 mL</u>

| Multiply 1000, just move the decimal point (.) 3 places to the right.
0.700 = 700 |

* <u>Note</u> – remember, every whole number has a decimal point on the far right.

Ex:

        s   L
1,279 ml = <u>1.279 L</u>

> Divide 1000, just move the decimal point (.) 3 places to the left.
> 1279. = 1.279

Ex:

    s   L
77 ml = <u>0.077 L</u>

> Divide 1000, just move the decimal point (.) 3 places to the left.
> 0077. = 0.077

Temperature

<u>U.S. Customary</u> units used in the measurement of temperature are degrees in Fahrenheit (F). Degrees are always shown with a <u>small</u> zero after the number of degrees and at the top, and then put the F.

32° F is the freezing point
212° F is the boiling point

<u>Metric</u> units used in the measurement of temperature are degrees in Celsius (C).

0° C is the freezing point
100° CF is the boiling point

Thermometers are used to register the temperature. These can be liquid or digital. Most thermometers show both Fahrenheit and Celsius readings.

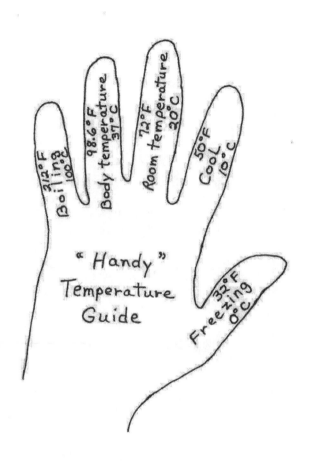

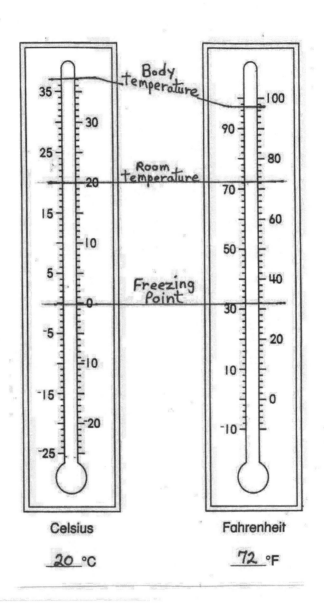

Figuring Temperatures and Changes

Any temperature below 0° on any kind of thermometer is registered as minus (-) before the temperature number. So – 6° C means 6 degrees below zero.

To figure how far a temperature has changed over time, simply <u>subtract</u> the beginning and ending temperatures if <u>BOTH</u> readings are either above zero <u>OR</u> <u>BOTH</u> below zero.

Ex:

      23° C to 34° C = 11°   (34 - 23)

      35° F to 21° F = 14°   (35 - 21)

      -5° C to -28° C = 23°   (28 - 5)

* <u>Note</u> – Notice that the answer does NOT have on F or a C after the degree "°". This is because the answer is showing how much the temperature has changed, not what the temperature is or has become.

If one is above 0° and one is below 0°, you must <u>add</u> to find the changes in temperature. If the temperature starts at -5° F in the morning and gets to 33° F in the afternoon, the temperature had to move up five degrees to zero and then continue 33 degrees more, so you add 5 + 33 = 38° to get a change of 38°.

If the temperature goes down due to bad weather, going from 5° C to -3° C, it had to move from 5 to zero and then continue to -3. So 5 + 3 = 8° change.

* <u>Note</u> – Showing this movement on a number line makes it easy to understand.

Time

The passage of time is measured the same universally.

Basic Units

1 minute	=	60 seconds
1 hour	=	60 minutes
1 day	=	24 hours
1 week	=	7 days
1 month	=	about 4 weeks, about 30 days
1 year	=	12 months = 52 weeks = 365 days
1 decade	=	10 years
1 century	=	100 years
1 millennium	=	1000 years

A year is really $365\frac{1}{4}$ days. Since we cannot have just one fourth of a day, every four years the $\frac{1}{4}$ days are added up to make $\frac{4}{4}$, which we know equals one whole day. That day then is added to the month of February, which is the shortest month with 28 days to make 29 days. We call this year **leap year**.

Days of each month

January	=	31
February	=	28 (29 in leap year)
March	=	31
April	=	30
May	=	31
June	=	30
July	=	31
August	=	31
September	=	30
October	=	31
November	=	30
December	=	31

An easy way to help you remember these is the following poem:

30 days has September, April, June and November. All the rest have 31 except for February which has 28 except for leap year it has 29.

Calculating and Converting Units of Time

The same rules apply using the basic units to go from large to small and from small to large.

Ex:

    L   S
  3 yrs = <u>36</u> months (mo)   (1 yr = 12 months) multiply

    L   S
  6 days = <u>144</u> hrs   (1 day = 24 hrs) multiply

    L   S
  4 yrs = <u>208</u> wks   (1 yr = 52 wks) multiply

Ex:

    S   L
  62 days = <u>8</u> wk <u>6</u> days   (1 wk = 7 days) divide

    S   L
  624 days = <u>1</u> yr <u>259</u> days   (1 yr = 365 days) divide

    S   L
  4759 sec = <u>1</u> hr <u>1159</u> sec   (1 hr = 3600 sec) divide
              1 hr <u>19</u> min <u>19</u> sec

Ex:

    L   S
  5 hr 29 min = <u>329</u> min   (1 hr = 60 min)
                           60 × 5 = 300 + 29 = 329

Elapsed Time

Elapsed time shows how much time has passed from one time of day to another time of day.

There are 24 hours in a whole day. It is divided in two parts:

1) AM – Midnight to noon
   12:00 AM - 12:00 PM (12 hours)

2) PM – Noon to midnight
   12:00 PM – 12:00 AM (12 hours)

Military Time does NOT split the day into two twelve hour parts. Military time starts at 12:00 midnight and continues counting to the next 12:00 midnight using numbers 1 through 24 hundred hours.

We will <u>Not</u> be using military time; we will be using AM and PM times.

AM – stands for <u>ante</u> <u>meridian,</u> which means <u>before</u> noon since meridiem means middle, so noon is the middle of the day.

PM – stands for <u>post</u> <u>meridian,</u> which means <u>after</u> the middle of the day.

If you are only dealing with the hours and both times are in the morning (AM) or in the afternoon (PM) or evening, simply add or subtract the hours.

Ex: How much time has elapsed?

From 9:00 AM to 11:00 AM is 2 hours.
11 – 9 = 2

Ex: What time will it be?

3 hours after 5:00 AM
5 + 3 = 8:00 AM

Proof! 5:00 – 6:00 – 7:00 – 8:00
             1 hr   1 hr   1 hr   (3 hrs)

Ex: What time will it be?

4 hours before 11:00 PM
11 – 4 = 7:00 PM

When dealing with hours and minutes, you may have to do some converting when adding or subtracting.

Remember 1 hour = 60 minutes

Ex:

20 min after 9:20 AM = 9:40 AM
(Simply add 20 + 20 = 40 since 40 is less than 60)

Ex: What time will it be?

   30 min after 7:50 PM?

Add the minutes: 30 + 50 = 80

Since 80 is greater than 60, you need to subtract 60 from 80 and change it into 1 hour and 20 minutes left.

   80
   -60 = 1 hr. (add to 7)
   20 min left

The answer becomes 8:20 PM

Ex: What time will it be 15 min before 2:05 AM?

You must change 2 hours to 1 hr 60 min plus 5 min = 1 hr 65 min. Now you can subtract 15 min.

   1:65
   - 15
   1:50 AM is the answer

When you are adding time from AM to PM, you must count the <u>full</u> hours and then add the minutes. You may have to also convert to the next hour.

Ex: How much time is between 7:40 AM to 3:45 PM?

   7:40 = 12:40 (afternoon) = 5 hrs
   12:40 – 3:40 (afternoon) = 3 hrs
   (45 – 40 = 5 min)   8 hrs 5 min

Adding and Subtracting Time

Ex:

      5 hr 22 min   8 hr 21 min
    + 2 hr 20 min   - 1 hr 15 min
      7 hr 42 min   7 hr 6 min

        9   +60
    ~~10~~ hrs 12 min = 9 hr 72 min
  -   7 hrs 36 min = 7 hr 36 min
                    2 hr 36 min

As you can see, you can't subtract 36 min from 12 min so we had to take 1 hr from 10 hrs, which leaves 9 hrs, and change it to 60 min and add 60 min to 12 min. This makes 72 min and now we can subtract.

Ex:

      4 hrs 25 min
   + 1 hr 52 min
      5 hrs 77 min
        - 60 min = 1 hr to add to 5 hrs
          17 min left

Answer becomes 6 hrs 17 min

Ex:
          4
      ~~5 hr~~   =   4 hrs 60 min
   - 2 hrs 37 min   =   - 2 hrs 37 min
                          2 hrs 23 min

Here again you can't subtract 37 min from nothing. You have to take 1 hr from 5 hrs to make it into 4 hrs and 60 min. Now you can subtract 37 min from 60 min.

Chapter 9:

GEOMETRY

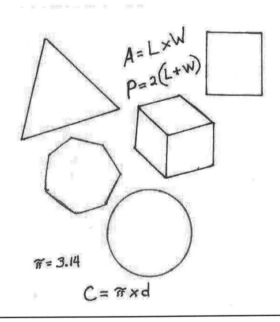

Geometric Models

1. **Line** – goes on and on forever in both directions

2. **The point**

3. **Line segment** – has a point to start at and end with

4. **Ray** – has a point at one end, but goes on and on at the other end

5. **A plane** – a flat surface, just like this paper

6. **Vertex** – the point on an angle where the two sides meet

7. **Right or square angle** – form a 90° angle at the vertex

8. **Intersecting lines** – where two lines cross

9. **Perpendicular** – lines that intersect and form 90° angles

10. **Parallel lines** – lines that never intersect

11. **Acute angle** – small angles that are less than 90°

12. **Obtuse angle** – any angle that is larger than 90°

13. **Vertices** – 2 or more vertex

14. **Angle** – two rays having the same endpoint

Symbols

1. Ray
2. ←——→ Line
3. ∠ Angle

Name this angle:

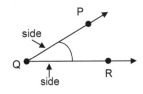

<PRQ

<RQP   Vertex must be in the center

Name this line:

 $\overleftrightarrow{AB}$

Shapes

Quadrilateral – a polygon with 4 sides, some quadrilaterals do not have 4 right angles.

Types of Quadrilaterals

1. **Square** – all sides have the same length and make 4 right angles.

2. **Rectangle** – opposite sides are parallel and the same length, it makes 4 right angles.

   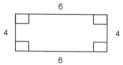

3. **Parallelogram** – 2 pairs of parallel sides with no right angles.

   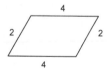

4. **Rhombus** – a parallelogram with sides that are all the same length.

5. **Trapezoid** – only 1 pair of parallel sides.

Shapes

Triangle – any 3 sided shape

1. **Equilateral triangle** – a triangle with three (3) equal sides.

2. **Isosceles triangle** – a triangle with two (2) equal sides.

3. **Scalene triangle** – a triangle with no equal sides.

4. **Right triangle** – a triangle that forms one (1) right or 90° angle.

5. **Acute triangle** – when all angles are less than 90°.

6. **Obtuse triangle** – when one angle measures more than 90°.

* <u>Note</u> – inside angles total 180° on <u>all</u> triangles.

Polygon – any shape with more than 2 sides.

1. **Mono (Uni)** – means one, like a unicycle

2. **Bi** – means two, like a bicycle

3. **Tri** – means three (3): Triangle △

4. **Quad** – means four (4): Quadrilateral ▱

5. **Penta** – means five (5): Pentagon ⬠

6. **Hexa** – means six (6): Hexagon ⬡

7. **Hepta** – means seven (7): Heptagon ⬡

8. **Octa** – means eight (8): Octagon (stop sign) ⬯

Comparing Shapes

Similar – Shapes that have the same shape, but they don't have the same size.

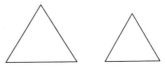

Congruent – Shapes that have the exact same <u>shape and size</u>.

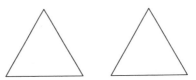

The only difference between congruent and similar is the size.

Pentomino – a figure made of 5 congruent (exactly the same) squares and joined or connected edge to edge, must share a side with its neighbor.

   Pentomino

   Not Pentomino's

Line of Symmetry – a line on which a figure can be folded so that the two parts fit exactly...the line MUST pass through the center of the object.

   Equal halves

A geometric space is the set of all points. A **geometric plane** is a set of points and is a subject of space. A **plane** is the surface of a flat object, such as this paper, a wall, your desk top, etc.

Plane geometry is the study of geometric shapes that include lines, angles, polygons, and circles. These are flat surfaces. Most objects you see will have a geometric shape, one or more of the polygon shapes.

Solid geometry are three-dimensional shapes such as a sphere (ball), cone, cube, rectangular prisms, pyramids, and cylinders.

Lines

The shortest distance between two points is a **straight line**. It has NO curve to it. Each line on your paper is a straight line. A straight line measures 180 degrees (180°).

This is half of a circle which measures 360°.

When you see a line with arrows at both ends, ←——→ , it means that the line continues in both directions with no end. To name a <u>line</u>, use the letters of the end points and put the line symbol ↔ above the letters.

Ex:

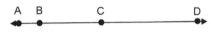

You read this line as line AD or line DA because these are the letters closest to the arrows.

AD or DA

* <u>Note</u> - notice the capital letter right next to each other and the line symbol above them.

Ex:

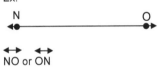

↔ ↔
NO or ON

A **line segment** is part of a line that has end points, NO arrows. The symbol for a line segment has NO arrows, just a line above the letters.

Ex:

F   G $\overline{FG}$ or $\overline{GF}$

This is read as line segment FG or line segment GF.

A **ray** is a line with only <u>one</u> arrow at one end and an end point at the other end. When you name a ray, you MUST start with the letter at the end point then the letter at the arrow. You can NOT reverse the letters. You must put the ray symbol ⟶ above the letters.

Ex:

S   T   = $\overrightarrow{ST}$ You read this as ray ST

Ex:

B   C   = $\overrightarrow{CB}$ ray CB

C must come first because C is next to the end point, NOT the arrow.

Parallel lines are two straight lines that <u>NEVER</u> meet. Think of railroad tracks, lines on your paper, top edge and bottom edge of a door, window, a picture frame, the right and left edge of your paper, etc. They are parallel to each other.

Ex:

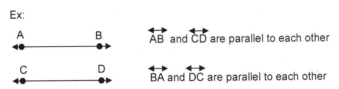

$\overleftrightarrow{AB}$ and $\overleftrightarrow{CD}$ are parallel to each other

$\overleftrightarrow{BA}$ and $\overleftrightarrow{DC}$ are parallel to each other

Intersecting lines are two lines that cross each other. Think of two roads that cross each other.

Ex:

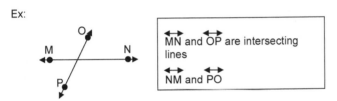

$\overleftrightarrow{MN}$ and $\overleftrightarrow{OP}$ are intersecting lines

$\overleftrightarrow{NM}$ and $\overleftrightarrow{PO}$

* <u>Note</u> – letters can be reversed because there are arrows at each end of each line.

Perpendicular lines are two intersecting lines that meet to form a right angle (90°). Think of the corners of a door or window, where the wall meets the ceiling in the corner of a room, the top or bottom corners of your paper, etc. These are perpendicular lines.

Ex:

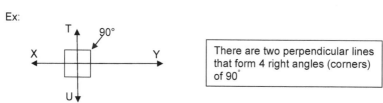

There are two perpendicular lines that form 4 right angles (corners) of 90°

TU and XY are perpendicular lines

Whenever you see a square box in a corner where two lines meet, it means the two lines that cross forms a right angle, the two lines are perpendicular.

Angles

Angles are formed when two straight lines intersect. The space where they cross forms an angle (the space in the corner). The point where the two lines meet is called the vertex.

Ex:

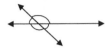

> The four spaces in the center form four angles

A **right angle** is formed by two perpendicular lines.

Ex:

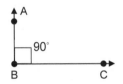

> A right angle ALWAYS measures 90°

Since we know that a circle has 360°, perpendicular lines form four right angles 90° each, 4 × 90° = 360°.

Ex:

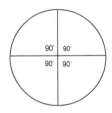

To name an angle, the point where the lines cross MUST be in the middle of the three letters because it is the **vertex**. Use the angle symbol < before the letters.

Ex:

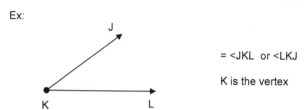

= <JKL or <LKJ

K is the vertex

This angle can also be named as angle K written as <K.

Use the following diagram to see how we answer the questions.

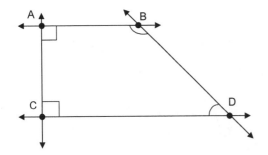

Name each figure:

1.) The rays that form <B

$\overrightarrow{BA}$ and $\overrightarrow{BD}$ (Must start with B because these are rays)

2.) The angle that has C as its vertex

<ACD or <DCA (C must be in the middle)

3.) Perpendicular line (remember they MUST make a right angle)

$\overleftrightarrow{AC}$ and $\overleftrightarrow{CD}$
$\overleftrightarrow{AB}$ and $\overleftrightarrow{AC}$

4.) Parallel lines (remember lines can't meet)

$\overleftrightarrow{AB}$ and $\overleftrightarrow{CD}$

Kinds of Angles

Angles are also named by their size.

1.) A **right angle** is formed by two perpendicular lines to make 90°.

Ex:

Right angle

2.) An **acute angle** is formed when two lines meet making an angle <u>LESS</u> than 90° (smaller than a right angle). An easy way to remember these is to think of them as "cuties".

Ex:

An <u>acute</u> angle, shaded area is smaller than the square box

45°

3.) An **obtuse angle** is formed by two lines that form an angle <u>GREATER</u> than 90° (larger than a right angle).

Ex:

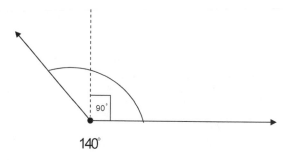

140°

An <u>obtuse</u> angle, curved area, is <u>larger</u> than the square box

Remember a straight line is 180°. A straight line is two right angles back to back.

Ex:

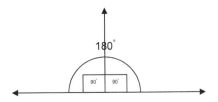

A **protractor** is an instrument used to measure the degrees in an angle.

Acute Angle = 45°
Obtuse Angle = 135°

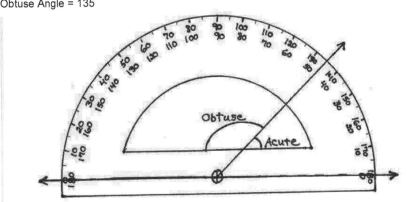

This center MUST be placed at the vertex.

The bottom edge of the protractor goes along the bottom of the angle. The other line of the angle crosses the protractor at a place with degrees either less than 90° or greater depending on the kind of angle. So if the angle is acute, you will use the smaller numbers as above. An obtuse angle uses the larger numbers.

Geometric Shapes

Polygons

Polygons are simple closed figures, no open spaces, <u>only</u> straight sides. All polygons have an exterior (<u>perimeter</u>), and an interior (<u>area</u>).

Polygons include, naming the most common shapes, triangles, quadrilaterals, pentagons, hexagons, and octagons.

All polygons are named for the number of their sides and the shape of their angles.

Triangles

Triangles – "tri" means 3 sides. Think of three letters in "tri". Triangles are classified by their angles and length of their sides.

Triangles by Angles

A **right triangle** has one right angle (90°).

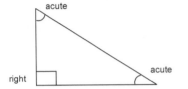

> One right triangle ▫ 90°
> Two acute angles that add up to 90°

An **acute triangle** has <u>three</u> acute angles (each less than 90°).

An **obtuse triangle** has <u>one</u> obtuse angle (larger than 90°) and two acute angles.

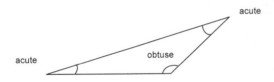

* <u>Note</u> – all three angles of a triangle must add up to 180°.

Triangles by sides

An **equilateral** triangle has three equal sides.

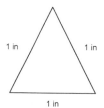

All sides are equal. All angles are acute.

An **isosceles** triangle has only two equal sides.

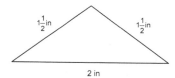

Two sides are equal.

A **scalene** triangle has NO equal sides, all are different.

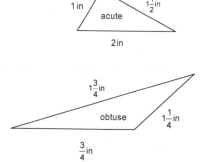

All sides are different.
All angles are different.

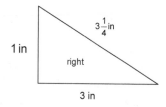

Quadrilaterals

Quad means 4 (4 letters). All **quadrilaterals** have 4 sides.

Types of Quadrilaterals

Rectangles – all have 4 sides, 4 right angles, opposite sides are equal in length and parallel to each other.

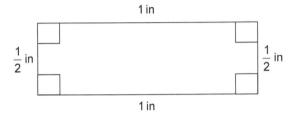

Square – a rectangle with all four sides equal.

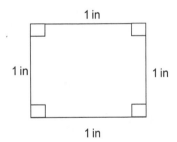

Parallelogram – 4 sides, opposite sides are equal and parallel, opposite angles are equal.

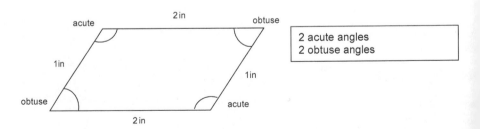

Rhombus – same as a parallelogram only all sides are equal in length.

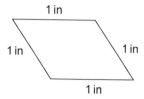

Do **NOT** call it a diamond

Trapezoid – 4 sides, only <u>one</u> pair of parallel lines.

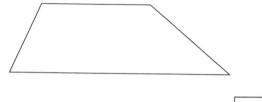

Top and bottom line of each of these examples are parallel

* <u>Note</u> – all four angles must add up to 360°.

Other Polygons

Pentagon – <u>penta</u> mean 5 (5 letters), 5 sides that are all equal.

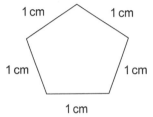

Hexagon – six equal sides. (Think of the word six. 3 letters, ends in x, <u>hex</u> has three letters, ends in x)

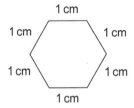

Octagon – eight equal sides and angles. Octo means 8. Think of an octopus with 8 legs, also the shape of a stop sign.

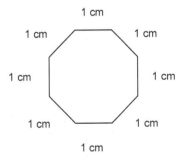

* <u>Note</u> – these are <u>regular</u> polygons meaning all sides are equal in length.

The following shapes are polygons because they are closed figures.

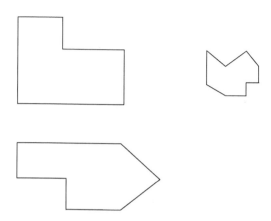

Below are samples of polygons and the sum of their inner angles.

(Number of sides - 2) × 180° = Sum of the angles

n	n − 2 × 180	Sum of the Angles
3	1 × 180	180°
4	2 × 180	360°
5	3 × 180	540°
6	4 × 180	720°
8	6 × 180	1080°

Perimeter

Perimeter is the <u>distance around</u> a polygon.

If all the sides are different length, simply add all of the sides. You must put the label of the units used.

Ex:

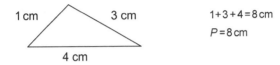

$1 + 3 + 4 = 8$ cm

$P = 8$ cm

If all the sides are equal, multiply the number of sides times the length of each side.

Ex:

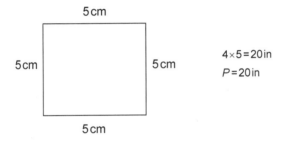

$4 \times 5 = 20$ in

$P = 20$ in

Formulas for Perimeter of Rectangles and Squares

Rectangle

L = length W = width

$P = 2 \times (L + W)$

$P = 2 \times (5 + 2)$

$P = 2 \times 7$

$P = 14$ ft

5 ft
2 ft   2 ft
5 ft

Square

s = side

$P = 4 \times s$

$P = 4 \times 3$

$P = 12$ cm

3 cm
3 cm   3 cm
3 cm

Converting Perimeter

Find the perimeter around a pool measuring 30 ft by 12 ft.

$P = 2 \times (L + W)$

$P = 2 \times (30 + 12)$

$P = 2 \times 42$

$P = 84$ ft

12 ft

30 ft

Convert 84 ft to yards by dividing by 3 since 3 ft equals 1 yard.

84 ft = 28 yds

```
    28
3)84
   -6
   24
  -24
    0
```

Find the perimeter of a picture frame measuring 2 ft 4 in by 1 ft 10 in.

$P = 2 \times (L + W)$

$P = 2 \times (2$ ft 4 in $+ 1$ ft 10 in$)$

$P = 2 \times (3$ ft 14 in$)$

$P = 6$ ft 28 in

1 ft 10 in

2 ft 4 in

Convert 6 ft 28 into yards, feet and inches by changing 6 ft to 2 yards, 28 in to 2 ft (24 in) and 4 in left over.

So, 6 ft 28 in = 2 yds 2 ft 4 in

Find the perimeter of a square measuring 16 in.

$P = 4 \times (16 \text{ in})$

$P = 64 \text{ in}$

16 in

Convert 64 inches into feet by dividing by 12 (12 in = 1 ft).

So, 64 in = 5 ft 4 in

```
      5
  12)64
     -60
       4
```

Area

Area is the amount of space <u>inside</u> a closed figure. This is measured in <u>square units</u>. The answer MUST include the word square. This can be abbreviated, sq, or written as a small ^{2} after the unit label. Ex: 24 ft^2, which means 24 square feet.

To find the <u>area of a rectangle</u>, use the formula $A = L \times W$ (<u>l</u>ength times <u>w</u>idth)

Ex:

    4 units

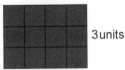

    3 units

$A = L \times W$
$A = 4 \times 3$
$A = 12$ sq units or 12 units^2

As you can see, there are 12 square boxes inside the rectangle.

* <u>Note</u> – remember, the perimeter is the distance around the outside.

$P = 2 \times (3 + 4)$
$P = 2 \times 7$
$P = 14$ units

As you can see, area gets <u>square</u> as part of its answer and perimeter does <u>NOT</u>.

If you don't put <u>square</u> (sq. or ^{2}) after the label in the answer for area, you are automatically turning your answer into perimeter instead of area.

Ex: $A = 9$ cm^2 is area, but $P = 9$ cm is perimeter.

Area of a Square uses the formula $A = s^2$ where s means side. Since all the sides are equal so you multiply one side by itself.

Ex:

$A = 3^2$
$A = 3 \times 3$
$A = 9$ cm^2

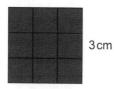

3 cm

As you can see, when you count all of the squares there are 9 squares, $3 \times 3 = 9$.

The perimeter of this square would be 12 cm.

$P = 4 \times 3$ (4 sides times 3)
$P = 12$ cm

Ex:

$A = L \times W$
$A = 4.5 \times 1.5$
$A = 6.75$ cm^2

1.5 cm

4.5 cm

Area of a Right Triangle

All triangles are half of a rectangle; therefore, you figure the area of the rectangle and divide by 2 (half).

Use the formula $A = \frac{1}{2} \times (b \times h)$

b is the base and h is the height.

These are the same as length and width.

Ex:

$A = \frac{1}{2} \times (3 \times 2)$

$A = \frac{1}{2} \times 6$

$A = 3 \, cm^2$

2 cm

3 cm

* Note – the dotted lines complete the rectangle, the shaded area is half of the rectangle.

Remember, if you don't put square (sq or ^{2}) in your answer, it will NOT be correct. You will turn it into perimeter instead of area.

Area of Other Triangles

The same formula is used for any triangle since all triangles are half of a rectangle.

$A = \frac{1}{2} \times (b \times h)$

Ex:

$A = \frac{1}{2} \times (b \times h)$

$A = \frac{1}{2} \times (5 \times 3)$

$A = \frac{1}{2} \times 15$

$A = 7.5\,cm^2$

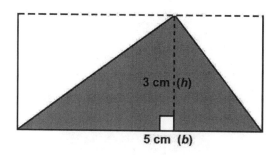

3 cm (h)

5 cm (b)

* <u>Note</u> – dotted line shows full rectangle. Dotted line down the inside of the triangle shows the height.

Using graph paper to make your triangles makes it very easy to see the full rectangle around the triangle and to count all the squares that make up the rectangle and the triangle.

Ex:

$A = \frac{1}{2} \times (7 \times 4)$

$A = \frac{1}{2} \times 28$

$A = 14\,cm^2$

4cm

7cm

* <u>Note</u> – dotted lines show the whole rectangle, there are 28 squares in the rectangle. Half is 14.

Area of Parallelograms

To figure the area of a parallelogram, you use the same formula as for a rectangle only substitute the L (length) for b (base) and the W (width) for h (height).

Rectangle   Parallelogram
A = L × W   A = b × h

Think of a parallelogram as a slanting rectangle, so if you could straighten it up, it would be a perfect rectangle.

Ex:

$A = b \times h$
$A = 8 \times 3$
$A = 24 \, in^2$

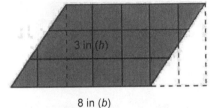
8 in (b)

* Note – dotted lines for rectangle

Ex:

$A = b \times h$
$A = 5 \times 3$
$A = 15 \, sq \, cm$

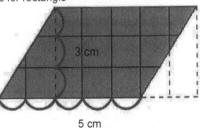
5 cm

* Note – perfect rectangle between dotted lines

Area of Other Polygons

Each square is a square (sq) unit. Two half squares equal one whole square unit. Count all the squares.

Ex:

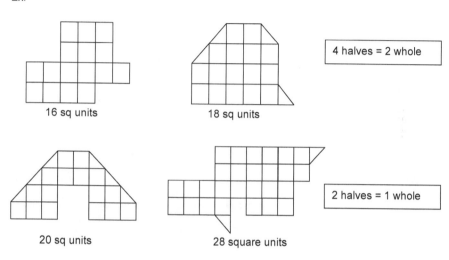

Circles and Circumference

A **circle** is a closed, curved line that has an outer edge that is the same distance from a center point ALL the way around measuring 360°.

This is a circle. No matter <u>where</u> you measure from, the center to circle line, it will be the same measurement. Think of a tire and its spokes.

This is NOT a circle. This is an oval. It is NOT the same distance from the center all around.

A circle is named by its center point.

Parts of a Circle

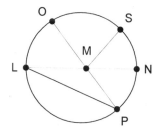

Circle M is the name of this circle.

1. A **diameter** is a straight line that goes from one side of a circle to the other side through the center point. LN is a diameter, OP is another diameter.

2. A **radius** is a straight line that goes from the center to the side of the circle. The above circle shows 5 radii (plural for radius); ML, MO, MN, MS, and MP. Notice that each one begins with M which is the center point.

3. A **chord** is any straight line that goes from one point on the circle to another point. It may or may not go through the center point. LP, OP, and LN are each chords.

4. An **arc** is any section on the curve of a circle between points. LO, OS, SN, NP and LP are all arcs.

Circumference

Circumference is the measurement around the circle. It is about three times (3×) the diameter or 6 times (6×) a radius.

To find the circumference of a circle, use the formula C = π × d

π is the symbol for the Greek letter Pi. Pi always equals 3.14, so you multiply the length of the diameter times 3.14.

$C = \pi \times 14$
$C = 3.14 \times 14$
$C = 43.96 \, cm$

14 cm

```
  3.14
×   14
──────
  1256
  3140
──────
 43.96
```

If they only give you a radius measurement, you must multiply by 2 to get a diameter.

$C = 2 \times (\pi \times 6)$
$C = 2 \times (3.14 \times 6)$
$C = 2 \times 18.84$
$C = 36.68 \, in$

6 in

* <u>Note</u> – you also can simply multiply 2 × 6 = 12, then multiply 12 × 3.14

If you are given the circumference and you are asked to find the diameter, you will have to divide by π (3.14) to the nearest hundredths.

Ex:

$C = 48$ mm
$d = 48 \div 3.14$
$d = 15.29$ mm

```
         15.286  = 15.29
 3.14)48.00.000
      -314
       1660
      -1570
        900
       -628
        2720
       -2512
         2080
        -1884
          196
```

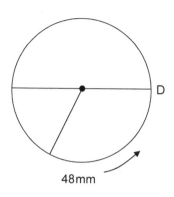

48mm

* <u>Note</u> – remember you MUST move the decimal point (.) two places to the <u>right</u> in both the divisor <u>AND</u> the dividend.

If you are given the circumference and are asked to find the radius, you must do the same as you did to find the diameter, but then you must divide by 2 since a radius is half the diameter.

Ex: Use the same example above:

$C = 48\,mm$
$r = (C \div \pi) \div 2$
$r = (48 \div 3.14) \div 2$
$r = 15.28 \div 2$
$r = 7.64\,mm$

```
       7.64
    2)15.28
     -14
      12
     -12
       8
     - 8
       0
```

Area of a Circle

The area (inside square units) of a circle can be found by using the formula $A = \pi r^2$ (area equals pi (3.14) times the radius squared).

Remember, when you square a number, you multiply it by itself, as in 4 × 4.

Ex:

$A = \pi r^2$
$A = 3.14 \times (6 \times 6)$
$A = 3.14 \times 36$
$A = 113.04 \, in^2$

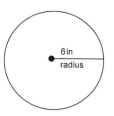

```
   3.14
 ×   36
  ─────
   1884
   9420
  ─────
 113.04
```

Ex:

$A = \pi r^2$
$A = 3.14 \times (3.5 \times 3.5)$
$A = 3.14 \times 12.25$
$A = 38.465 \, cm^2$
    or $38.5 \, cm^2$ to the nearest tenth

```
    12.25
  ×  3.14
  ──────
     4900
    12250
   367500
  ───────
  38.4650
```

$D = 7$
$r = 7 \div 2$
$r = 3.5$

```
    3.5
 ×  3.5
  ─────
    175
   1050
  ─────
  12.25
```

Similar and Congruent Figures

Congruent figures are shapes that have the <u>SAME</u> <u>SHAPE</u> <u>AND</u> <u>SIZE</u>. One can perfectly match the other (mirror image).

Tracing paper or patty paper is very useful in seeing if two polygons are congruent.

Similar figures or polygons can be congruent <u>OR</u> one can be smaller but <u>MUST</u> be the <u>SAME</u> <u>SHAPE</u>.

Tracing paper or patty paper can also be used to see if two polygons are similar.

Similar
<u>Same</u> shape but <u>different</u> size

Congruent
<u>Same</u> shape and size

<u>Not</u> congruent or similar
Have different shape

Congruence and Motion

Pentominos are <u>five</u> square shapes that share sides.

Ex:

      Pentomino   <u>NOT</u> a Pentomino

These can be used to show motions of rotation (turn), reflection (flip), and translation (slide) of congruent figures.

Ex: **rotation** movement (turn)

Ex: **reflection** (flip) (mirror image)

Ex: **translation** (slide)

Symmetry

Symmetrical shapes can be divided equally into two or more identical parts, mirror images.

When you fold a piece of paper in half so the corners meet perfectly, you now have two congruent parts. The fold becomes a **line of symmetry**.

To make a perfect Valentine heart, fold a piece of paper in half, from the fold cut half a heart. When you open it up, you will have a whole heart.

Folded

A square has four lines of symmetry: horizontal, vertical, and two diagonals. Each time you fold on the dotted lines, you will get two congruent halves.

A rectangle has only two lines of symmetry, horizontal and vertical.

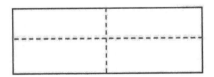

If there are **NO** lines of symmetry, then the figure is **asymmetrical**.

Ex:

No matter how you divide this cup shape, the two halves will **NOT** match.

A **regular polygon** means that all of the sides are equal; therefore, the number of lines of symmetry will match the number of sides or vertices.

Ex:

3 sides = 3 lines of symmetry

Equilateral triangle

Ex:

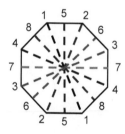

8 sides = 8 lines of symmetry

Octagon

Ex:

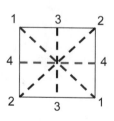

4 sides = 4 lines of symmetry

Square

Geometric Solids

Geometric solids are <u>three-dimensional</u>, meaning that they are not flat geometric shapes like this sheet of paper. They have depth besides length, width, or height. A box or cube is an example of a geometric solid.

A **prism** has a flat top like a box.

A **pyramid** comes to a point at the top.

Geometric solids are named by the number of their <u>sides</u> which are called <u>faces</u> and <u>bases</u>. A base is usually at the top or bottom.

Vertices (plural for vertex) are the points or corners where the sides meet.

Edges are the full long end of a side where it connects to another side.

Prisms

Prisms have <u>flat</u> tops and are named by the shape of their bases.

Triangular Prism

Bases:	2 (triangular ends)
faces:	3 (lettered rectangles)
vertices:	6 (circled corners)
edges:	9 (numbered lines)

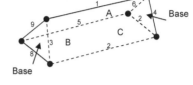

Rectangular Prism

Bases:	2 (top and bottom)
faces:	4 (lettered front, back, 2 sides)
vertices:	8 (circled corners)
edges:	12 (numbered lines)

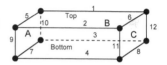

<u>Cube</u> – square prism, all sides are equal, all the same parts as rectangular prism.

Pentagonal Prism (5 sides)

Bases:	2 (top and bottom)
faces:	5 (lettered sides)
vertices:	10 (circled corners)
edges:	15 (numbered lines)

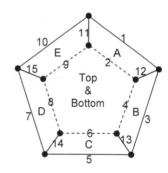

Hexagonal Prism (6 sides)

Bases: 2 (top and bottom)
faces: 6 (lettered sides)
vertices: 12 (circled corners)
edges: 18 (numbered lines)

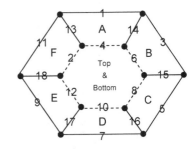

Octagonal Prism (8 sides)

Bases: 2 (top and bottom)
faces: 8 (lettered sides
vertices: 16 (circled corners)
edges: 24 (numbered lines)

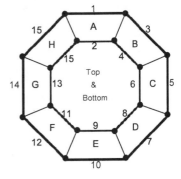

* <u>Note</u> – edges equal 3 times the number of faces, vertices equal 2 times the number of faces.

Pyramids

Pyramids must come to a point at the top. They are named by the shape of the bases.

Triangular Pyramid

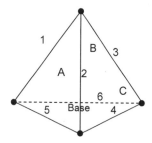

- bases – 1 (triangular bottom)
- vertices – 4 (circled corners)
- faces – 3 (lettered sides)
- edges of base – 3 (numbers 4, 5, 6)
- total edges – 6 (numbered lines)

Rectangular Pyramid

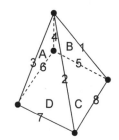

- bases – 1 (rectangular bottom)
- vertices – 5 (circled corners)
- faces – 4 (lettered sides)
- edges of base – 4 (numbers 5, 6, 7, 8)
- total edges – 8 (numbered lines)

* Note – total number of edges equals 2 times the number of edges of the base.

Exploring Surface Area

To figure the surface area of a rectangular prism, use the formula surface area (*SA*), equals two times the front area (*FA*), plus two times the side area (*SA*) plus two times the top area (*TA*).

SA = (2 × FA) + (2 × SA) + (2 × TA)

* <u>Note</u> – front area = front and back (same sizes)
           side area = right and left ends (same sizes)
           top area = top and bottom (same sizes)

<u>Remember</u> area = length times width or base times height

Ex:

$SA = (2 \times FA) + (2 \times SA) + (2 \times TA)$
$SA = (2 \times 40) + (2 \times 15) + (2 \times 24)$
$SA = 80 + 30 + 48$
$SA = 158 \, cm^2$

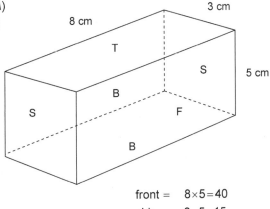

front = 8×5=40
side = 3×5=15
top = 8×3=24

Surface Area for a Cube

A cube has <u>all</u> sides equal. Since there are 6 equal sides, simply figure the area of one side and multiply by 6.

Area of the top equals 16 in².

$SA = 6 \times 16$ in²
$SA = 96$ in²

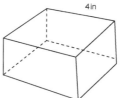

To figure the surface area of a <u>triangular prism</u> or <u>triangular pyramid</u>, you must use the formula for the area of a triangle to figure the triangular sides then add the sides.

Remember, a triangle is $\frac{1}{2}$ a rectangle.

Ex: 2 ends are triangles
Area of 1 triangle

$A = (6 \times 5) \div 2$
$A = 30 \div 2$
$A = 15$ ft²

2 ends equal 30 ft²

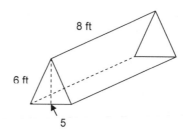

Ex: Area of all three faces are the same

$A = 6 \times 8 = 48$
3 sides times $48 = 144$

$SA = 30 + 144$
$SA = 174$ ft²

Volume

Volume is how many cubic units will fit inside an object. To show cubic units, a small 3 is put after the measurement label.

For the following, you can count how many cubes are on the top row, then multiply that by how many rows there are, or use the formula $V = L \times W \times h$. (h = height)

Ex:

(8 on top)
(3 rows)

$V = (4 \times 2) \times 3$

$V = 8 \times 3$

$V = 24$ cubic units

or

24 units^3

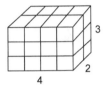

Ex:

(12 on top)
(5 rows)

$V = (4 \times 3) \times 5$

$V = 12 \times 5$

$V = 60 \text{ units}^3$

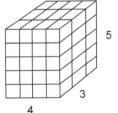

Ex:

(9 on top)
(4 rows)

$V = (3 \times 3) \times 4$

$V = 9 \times 4$

$V = 36 \text{ units}^3$

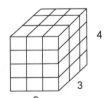

Ex:

$V = (5 \times 3) \times 3$
$V = 15 \times 3$
$V = 45 \text{ units}^3$

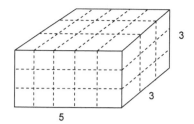

Ex:

$V = (6 \times 4) \times 2$
$V = 24 \times 2$
$V = 48 \text{ cm}^3$

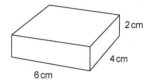

Ex:

$V = (2 \times 5) \times 4$
$V = 10 \times 4$
$V = 40 \text{ in}^3$

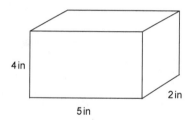

Volume Formulas

Volume of:

1. Rectangular prism – $L \times W \times h$ (lenght times width times height)

2. Cube – s^3 (side times side times side)

3. Pyramid - $\dfrac{B \times h}{3}$ (base times height divided by 3)

4. Cylinder - $B \times h$ (base times height)
   $\pi r^2 \times h$ (pi (3.14) times radius squared times height)

5. Cone - $\dfrac{B \times H}{3}$ (base times height divided by 3)

   $\dfrac{\pi r^2 \times h}{3}$ (pi (3.14) times radius squared times height divided by 3)

6. Sphere - $\dfrac{4\pi r^3}{3}$ (4 times pi (3.14) times radius cubed divided by 3)

Connecting Metric Volume, Mass, and Capacity

Volume is how many cubic units fit inside.

Mass is weight of volume.

Capacity is how much liquid fill the volume.

Volume = amt of liquid (L) = amt of liquid (mL) = mass (kg) = mass (g)

Think of an aquarium measuring 45 cm long, 20 cm wide, and the water level at 20 cm high.

Ex:

$V = (45 \times 20) \times 20$
$V = 900 \times 20$
$V = 18,000 \, cm^3$ Volume = Capacity = Mass
              $(1000 \, cm^3 = 1 \, L = 1000 \, mL = 1 \, kg = 1000 \, g)$

So, for the above aquarium

V   =   Capacity   =   Mass
                liters = milliliters   kilograms = grams

$18,000 \, cm^3$ = 18L = 18,000 mL = 18 kg = 18,000 g

Ex:

$V = (20 \times 25) \times 10$
$V = 500 \times 10$
$V = 5,000 \, cm^3$

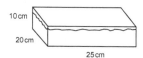

V   = L =   mL = kg = g

$5000 \, cm$ = 5 L = 5000 mL = 5 kg = 5000 g

Nautical Measures

Nautical measures are used for distance and depth at sea.

Distance

cable	= 0.1 nautical mile
nautical mile	= 6.076 feet or 1,852 meters
marine league	= 3 nautical miles (5.6 kilometers)

Circular Distance

degree	= 60 nautical miles

Depth

fathom	= 60 nautical miles 6 feet or 1.83 meters
mark	= fathoms marked on a sounding line

Speed

knot	= 1 nautical mile per hour

Light Year

Distances in space are so vast that they are too great to measure by miles. Scientists have used a system called Light Years to show distance. Light travels at the speed of 186,282 miles per second. So, one Light Year equals 5.878 trillion miles or 9.5 trillion kilometers.

Our sun is about 93 million miles from the earth. It takes about 8 minutes for the light rays of the sun to reach the earth.

Astronomical Units (AU) were developed by scientists to measure distance within our solar system. The distance from earth to the sun is 92.9 million miles or 1 astronomical unit (AU).

Average distances from the sun:

Mercury	=	0.04 AU
Venus	=	0.07 AU
Earth	=	1.00 AU
Mars	=	1.50 AU
Jupiter	=	5.20 AU
Saturn	=	9.60 AU
Uranus	=	19.20 AU
Neptune	=	30.10 AU
Pluto	=	39.40 AU

Chapter 10:

RATIO AND PROBABILITY

Ratios

A **ratio** shows the comparison between two quantities.

The two numbers used in a ration <u>must</u> be given in the same kinds of units.

Ex: money to money or dogs to puppies, etc.

The first number is called the <u>first term</u> and the second number is called the <u>second term</u>.

A ration can be written three ways:

1. The word <u>to</u> between the two numbers

    Ex: 1 to 4

2. As a fraction

    Ex: $\frac{1}{4}$

3. A colon (:) between the two numbers

    Ex: 1:4

All three are read as, one is to four.

Ex:
    Comparing 2 kittens and 3 cats
    2 to 3, $\frac{2}{3}$, 2:3

Ex:
    Compare $3 and $10
    $3 to $10, $\frac{\$3}{\$10}$, $3:$10

* <u>Note</u> – whichever unit is written first or shown first, MUST come first in the ratio.

Patterns in Ratio Tables

Making a ratio table is done the same way you would make equivalent fractions.

Remember to make equivalent fractions, simply multiply or divide <u>BOTH</u> numerator and denominator by the same number.

Ex:

$\dfrac{3}{4} = \dfrac{6}{8}$ Both 3 and 4 are multiplied by 2

Do the same to make a ratio table.

Ex:

3	6	9	12	15	18
4	8	12	16	20	24

For a table, always go to the first ratio to complete the rest or find the missing ratio numbers.

From above:

$\dfrac{3^{\times 2}}{4_{\times 2}} = \dfrac{6}{8} \qquad \dfrac{3^{\times 4}}{4_{\times 4}} = \dfrac{12}{16} \qquad \dfrac{3^{\times 6}}{4_{\times 6}} = \dfrac{18}{24}$

Each one is read as 3 to 4, 6 to 8, 9 to 12, 12 to 16, 15 to 20, 18 to 24.

If you are given a larger ratio and you are asked to give an equivalent ratio, think of a number that will go into both parts and divide.

Ex:

$\dfrac{10^{\div 5}}{45_{\div 5}} = \dfrac{2}{9} \qquad \dfrac{36^{\div 6}}{42_{\div 6}} = \dfrac{6}{7}$

If you are given a table with missing ration numbers, look at the first ratio (if given) and think of what you can multiply to get the ratio number that is there above or below the missing number and do the same to the other number in the first ratio. This will give you the missing number.

Ex:

3	6	9	12	15
5	10	15	20	25

Circled ones were missing.

$$\frac{3^{\times 2}}{5_{\times 2}} = \frac{6}{10} \qquad \frac{3^{\times 3}}{5_{\times 3}} = \frac{9}{15} \qquad \frac{3^{\times 5}}{5_{\times 5}} = \frac{15}{25}$$

If a whole ratio is missing in a table, look at the ratios before and after the missing one to see what can be multiplied to get the missing ratio.

Ex:

4	8	12	16
11	22	33	44

Circled ones were missing.

$$\frac{4^{\times 2}}{11_{\times 2}} = \frac{8}{22} \qquad \frac{4^{\times 4}}{11_{\times 4}} = \frac{16}{44}$$

So multiply 4 and 11 by 3

$$\frac{4^{\times 3}}{11_{\times 3}} = \frac{12}{33}$$

Equal Ratios on a Graph (Coordinates)

Equal ratios are also called **ordered pairs** and **coordinates**.

When plotting points on a graph using ordered pairs, the first term is always along the x axis (bottom) and the second term is along the y axis (left side) of the graph. You <u>always</u> go along the bottom to the first term number and then go up for the second term number. Think of an airplane. It must taxi down the runway gathering speed before it can go up into the air.

Ordered pairs are written as (1, 2), (2, 4), (3, 6), (4, 8). The first number is across the bottom, and the second number is on the left side.

So (1, 2) = 1 along the bottom, 2 up – put point where the two numbers meet

So (2, 4) = go to 2 on bottom, up to 4

So (3, 6) = go to 3 on bottom, up to 6

So (4, 8) = go to 4 on bottom, up to 8

When you connect the points, they make a straight line.

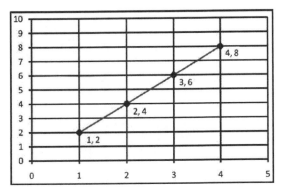

Plot ordered pairs on the graph.

1. (1, 3), (2, 6), (3, 9), (4, 12)

2. (6, 2), (12, 4), (18, 6)

Straight line shows that those ratios are equivalent.

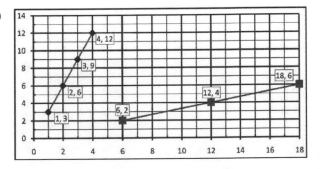

On a map, ordered pairs are coordinates. Every map shows the latitude and longitude lines that form a grid. This is extremely important in finding locations of places, ships, planes, cities, etc... The GPS, which mean global positioning system, uses these coordinates to find locations.

Probability

Probability is the likeliness (chances or odds) of something happening.

In a weather report, they might say there is a 30% chance of rain. This means a 30% change of rain and a 70% chance that it won't rain. So it is more likely that it won't rain. Or it is less likely that it will rain.

If it's an 80% chance of rain, it is more likely that it will rain compared to 20% that it won't. Either way, it is not 100% that it will rain.

50% chance of rain means it is equally likely that it will rain, 50% chance that it will not rain.

Equally likely is fair. Not equally likely is unfair.

If two people are playing a game, and each player has the same number of turns, then the game is fair. Each player has an equally likely chance to win.

If one player gets more turns than the other player, then the game is unfair because the player with the fewer turns is less likely to win.

Games of probability usually involve a spinner or dice (numbered cubes).

Ex:

Spin the spinner. Outcomes: 1, 2, 3, 4. Equally likely – fair. All spaces are different.

Ex:

Spin the spinner. Outcomes: 1, 3, 4. <u>Not</u> equally likely – unfair. All the spaces are <u>NOT</u> different. If points are awarded to each number, a player landing on 3 gets 6 points, but a player who lands on 4 only gets 4 points and if a player lands on 1, only gets one point. <u>Not</u> fair.

Ex:
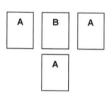

Draw a card. Outcome: A or B. But it is more likely that you will draw an A since there are 3 A's and only one B. This is unfair.

Predicting Outcomes

A bag contains red, green and yellow beads. Three samples are in the boxes below.

Ex: How many are there all together?
(Add all numbers in all sample bags)

74

Sample 1 bag
10 red
9 green
3 yellow

Ex: How many red are in all the samples?
(Add all the reds)

25 so 25 out of 74

about $33\frac{1}{3}$% or $\frac{1}{3}$ chance

Sample 2 bag
9 red
13 green
6 yellow

Ex: How many yellow are in all the samples?
(add all the yellows)

13 so 13 out of 74

about $\frac{1}{6}$ chance

Sample 3 bag
6 red
14 green
4 yellow

Ex: How many green are there?

36 so 36 out of 74
about 50% chance

Ex: What color would you predict as the <u>most likely</u> to pick?

Green

Ex: What color would you predict as the <u>least likely</u> to pick?

Yellow

Tree Diagrams for Probabilities

A tree diagram is one way to show all the possible outcomes in a probability problem.

Problem: Tina has in her closet several items that can be interchangeable outfits; blue skirt, white shorts, jeans, pink shirt, yellow sweater, sneakers, short boots.

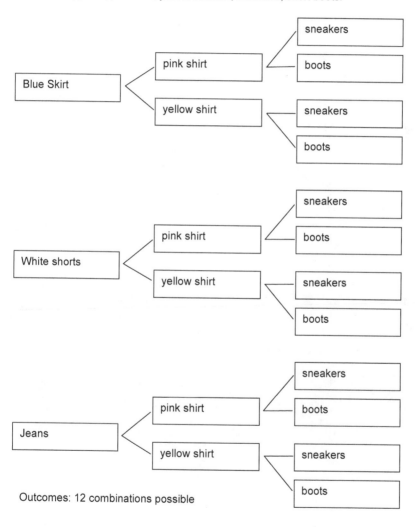

Outcomes: 12 combinations possible

Expressing Probability as Fractions

Probability is the ratio of favorable outcomes to the total outcomes. Ratios can be written as a fraction and simplified if needed.

Probability or ratio chosen:

1. Cherry: $\dfrac{5}{54}$ 5 out of 54 or 5 to 54

2. Apple: $\dfrac{15}{54} = \dfrac{5}{18}$ 5 to 18

3. Grape: $\dfrac{8}{54} = \dfrac{4}{27}$ 4 to 27

4. Blueberry: $\dfrac{11}{54}$ 11 to 54

5. Watermelon: $\dfrac{9}{54} = \dfrac{1}{6}$ 1 to 6

6. Orange: $\dfrac{6}{54} = \dfrac{1}{9}$ 1 to 9

Jolly Ranchers	# Chosen
Cherry	5
Apple	15
Grape	8
Blueberry	11
Watermelon	9
Orange	6
Total	54

What is the probability that a person will buy each?

1. tomatoes: $\dfrac{12}{36} = \dfrac{1}{3}$ 1 to 3

2. potatoes: $\dfrac{9}{36} = \dfrac{1}{4}$ 1 to 4

3. peppers: $\dfrac{6}{36} = \dfrac{1}{6}$ 1 to 6

4. onions: $\dfrac{3}{36} = \dfrac{1}{12}$ 1 to 12

5. celery: $\dfrac{2}{36} = \dfrac{1}{18}$ 1 to 18

6. carrots: $\dfrac{4}{36} = \dfrac{1}{9}$ 1 to 9

Vegetables	# Chosen
tomatoes	12
potatoes	9
peppers	6
onions	3
celery	2
carrots	4
Total	36

What are the odds (chances)?
(Likely and unlikely) (Certain or impossible)

Ex: Circle has 8 equal sized shapes

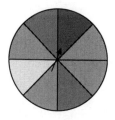

What are the chances a person would spin?

1. dark gray – $\frac{4}{8} = \frac{1}{2}$ 50% chance

2. black – $\frac{1}{8}$ 1 out of 8 chance

3. white – $\frac{1}{8}$ 1 out of 8 chance

4. light gray – $\frac{2}{8} = \frac{1}{4}$ 1 out of 4 chance, 25%

Ex: What is the probability of the spinner stopping on black or white? (You need to add both numbers of each of these colors.) Since there is only one of each, you have 2 out of 8, $\frac{2}{8} = \frac{1}{4}$ or 25% and because there is only one of each, there is an equally likely chance of picking black or white.

Ex:

1. What is the probability of the spinner stopping on 3?
    $\frac{0}{5}$ impossible

2. What are the odds the spinner will stop on 1?
    $\frac{1}{5}$ less likely

3. What are the odds the spinner will stop on 1, 2, 5, or 6?
    $\frac{5}{5}$ certain

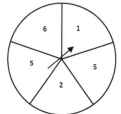

Chapter 11:

PRE-ALGEBRA

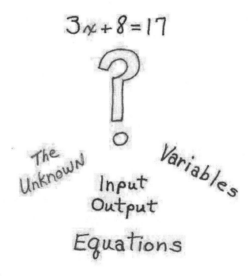

Integers
(Number System for <u>Algebra</u>)

An **integer** is any positive number or negative number beginning with zero. Positive integers are more than zero and negative integers are less than zero. The opposite number is found in the same position above or below zero on a number line.

3 below zero is written as -3. Its opposite is 3. (3 above zero)

Think of a thermometer, minus 5°F (-5°F) is 5 degrees below zero, 70°F is 70° above zero.

Absolute Values

The **absolute value** of a number is the distance from zero in either direction. Absolute value sign is $|n|$.

Number	Absolute Value
$|4|$	4
$|0|$	0
$|-5|$	5
$|-3|$	3

Inverse Property of Addition

Inverse property of addition is any number and its opposite.

-3 + 3 = 0   3 + -3 = 0
7 + -7 = 0   -7 + 7 = 0

If you start at negative 3 (-3) and then up 3, you will stop on zero.

If you start at positive 7 and then go down 7, you will stop at zero.

Adding Integers

If both numbers are negative, move to the left from zero on the number line.
(-2) + (-4) = -6

Do the same if both numbers are positive, moving to the right from zero on the number line.
3 + 5 = 8

If one number is positive and one is negative, start with the first number on the number line and then move to the opposite side of the zero to get to the second number. The answer will be the number you land on.

Ex:
5 + (-6) = -1

Start at 5 on the positive side and go to the left 6 places. You stop at -1.

Ex: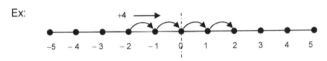

(-2) + 4 = 2

Start at (-2) and move 4 places to the right, you stop on 2 above zero.

When adding more than 2 integers, use the associative property whenever possible to make it easier. Remember, addition is <u>commutative</u> so the order of addends doesn't affect the sum.

Ex: (-5) + (-4) + 6

    (-4 + 6) + (-5)   or   (-4) + (6 + -5)
      2 + (-5)   (-4) + 1
        -3   -3

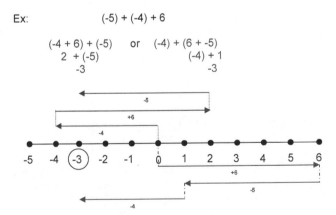

Subtracting Integers

To subtract integers, change the subtraction problem to an addition problem. Then change the second number to its opposite. So -2 becomes 2, 2 becomes -2.

Ex:
$$1 - 5 = 1 + (-5) = -4 \qquad \text{(-5 is opposite of 5)}$$

Start at 1, go left 5 spaces and stop at (-4).

Ex:
$$(-2) - (-4) = (-2) + 4 = 2 \qquad \text{(4 is opposite of -4)}$$

Start at (-2), go right 4 spaces and stop at 2.

Ex:
$$(-3) - (-3) = (-3) + 3 = 0 \qquad \text{(3 is the opposite of -3)}$$

Start at (-3), go right 3 spaces and stop at 0.

Ex:
$$(-4) - 3 = (-4) + (-3) = (-7) \qquad \text{(-3 is the opposite of 3)}$$

Start at (-4), go left 3 spaces and stop at (-7).

Multiplying of Integers

Rule #1: When you multiply two positive numbers, the product will be positive.

    Ex: 3 × 4 = 12
        (+) (+)   (+)

Rule #2: When you multiply two negative numbers, the product will be positive.

    Ex: (-8) × (-3) = (-24)
        (-)   (-)   (-)

Rule #3: When you multiply a positive number by a negative number, the product will be negative.

    Ex: 6 × (-2) = (-12)
        (+)   (-)   (-)

    Ex: (-5) × 3 = (-15)
        (-)   (+)   (-)

Division of Integers

Rule #1: When a positive number is divided by a positive number, the quotient will be positive.

    Ex: $36 \div 9 = 4$
         (+)   (+) (+)

Rule #2: When a negative number is divided by a negative number, the quotient will be positive.

    Ex: $(-36) \div (-9) = 4$
         (-)   (-) (+)

Rule #3: When a positive number is divided by a negative number, the quotient will be negative.

    Ex: $49 \div (-7) = (-7)$
         (+)   (-)   (-)

Rule #4: When a negative number is divided by a positive number, the quotient will be negative.

    Ex: $(-49) \div 7 = (-7)$
         (-)   (+) (-)

Variables
Algebraic Expressions

You have been working with algebraic expressions forever! A **variable** is any symbol that represents a missing number in a problem. It is the <u>unknown</u>. This is the part of the problem that you have to figure out, the <u>solution</u>. The variable can be in any part of the <u>arithmetic sentence</u> (algebraic expression).

Ex:
$23 - \square = 5$ $\square$ the box is the variable (unknown)

Ex:
$6 \times 4 = x$ x is the variable (unknown)

Ex:
$a \div 4 = 9$ a is the variable (unknown)

The value of the expression depends on the value of the variable.

In ALL math expressions, the = (equal sign) means that <u>BOTH</u> sides of the equal sign has the <u>SAME</u> <u>VALUE</u>. Each side can be very different, but when you figure out both sides, the values will be the <u>same.</u>

Ex:

$(3 + 6) - 2 = 10 - 3$
$9 - 2 = 7$
$7 = 7$

Both side of the = sign are different.

Final answer shows both sides = 7

Function Tables

Use a rule at the top of the table to figure out the input or output.

Ex:

(1 × 3) + 2 = 5

(2 × 3) + 2 = 8

(3 × 3) + 2 = (11)

(4 × 3) + 2 = (14)

Rule	× 3 + 2
Input	Output
1	5
2	8
3	?
4	?

Ex:

(1 × 6) ÷ 2 = 6

(2 × 6) ÷ 2 = (6)

(3 × 6) ÷ 2 = 9

(4 × 6) ÷ 2 = (12)

Rule	× 6 ÷ 2
Input	Output
1	3
2	?
3	9
4	?

Ex:

(3 × 8) - 5 = (19)

(4 × 8) - 5 = (27)

(5 × 8) - 5 = 35

(6 × 8) - 5 = 43

Rule	× 8 - 5
Input	Output
3	?
4	?
5	35
6	43

If you have to find the rule of the function table, you must look at the inputs and outputs to figure out the pattern to go from the input to the output.

Rule	?
Input	Output
2	6
4	12
6	18
8	24
10	30

Ask yourself what you have to do to go from the input to the output. Does it work for ALL of them?

Yes: 2 × 3 = 6
4 × 3 = 12
6 × 3 = 18
8 × 3 = 24
10 × 3 = 30

Rule is × 3

Rule	?
Input	Output
14	6
15	7
16	8
20	12
26	18

Ask yourself how to go from 14 to 6.

14 − □ = 6   15 − □ = 7   16 − □ = 8   20 − □ = 12
14 − 8 = 6   15 − 8 = 7   16 − 8 = 8   20 − 8 = 12

26 − □ = 18
26 − 8 = 18

Rule is -8

Multi-Function Rule

Rule	$(2 \times W) + (2 \times L) + 4$	
W	L	Output
4	7	26
8	12	44
12	20	68
16	24	84
20	30	104

$(2 \times 4) + (2 \times 7) + 4$

  8 + 14   + 4 = 26

$(2 \times 16) + (2 \times 24) + 4$

  32 + 48   + 4 = 84

Understanding and Writing Equations

Sometimes it may seem confusing in figuring out how to write an equation from the information given in a word problem. The following are many different ways you may see word problems information.

1. Twenty is five more than x

    $20 = x + 5$

2. Sixteen is half of x

    $16 = x \div 2$ or $16 = \dfrac{x}{2}$

3. x decreased by ten is thirty two

    $x - 10 = 32$

4. Two more than twice x is twenty

    $2x + 2 = 20$

5. Fifty six is twelve less than x

    $56 = x - 12$

6. The quotient of x and 3 is 9

    $x \div 3 = 9$ or $\dfrac{x}{3} = 9$

7. The product of six and x is 24

    $6x = 24$

8. The sum of x and eighteen is forty

    $x + 18 = 40$

9. The difference of x and twenty five is sixty three

    $x - 25 = 63$

10. One number is six times another

    $x = 6y$

11. One number is nine less than another

    $x = 7 - 9$

12. The sum of three consecutive whole numbers is twenty one

    $x + (x + 1) + (x + 2) = 21$

13. One number is five more than another

    $n = x + 5$

14. Six more than twice a number is 30

    $2x + 6 = 30$

15. Four times a number is fourteen more than three times the number

    $4x = 3x + 14$

16. Forty decreased by a number is three times the number

    $40 - x = 3x$

In an expression, when a number is right next to a variable, as in 4x, the number is known as a <u>coefficient</u> of the variable. 4x means 4 times the value of the variable. In 4x +3, 4x and 3 are both called the <u>terms</u> of the expression.

4x and 2x are <u>like</u> terms because they have the same variable.

In 4x + 6, each is an <u>unlike</u> term because they do not have the same variable. Only one of them has a variable.

To simplify expressions, like terms can be combined.

Ex: if x = 10, b = 3

$5x - 3b - 3x$
$(5x - 3x) - 3b$
$\quad 2x - 3b$
$(2 \times 10) - (3 \times 3)$
$\quad 20 \; - \; 9 \; = 11$

If an expression has parenthesis, use the distributive property to remove them.

Ex:

$\quad -(2 - 3m)$ = think minus (-) sign means -1

$\quad -1 (2 - 3m)$ = put -1 in place of –

$\quad -1 (2) = -1 (-3m)$ = -1 (2) means -1 × 2 = -2, and -1 (-3) mean -1 × (-3) = 3m

$\quad -2 + 3m$

Substituting Values for Variables

Ex: $x = 3$ $n = -2$

Substitute values of the variables

$2(x - 4) - 3(5 + m) = ?$
$2(3 - 4) - 3(5 + -2)$
$2(-1) - 3(3)$
$-2 - 9 = -11$

Ex: $a = 4$

Substitute value of the variable

$-(6 + a) + 2a = ?$
$-(6 + 4) + 2(4)$
$-10 \quad + 8 \quad = -2$

Ex: $y = 3$

Substitute value of the variable

$-(7y + 2) + 4y = ?$
$-(7\boxed{3} + 2) + 4(3)$
$-(21 + 2) \quad + 12 \quad = -11$
$\quad -23 \qquad + 12 \quad = -11$

Solving Equations with Like Terms (Variables)

Remember that an equal sign (=) means that <u>both</u> sides have the same <u>value</u>.

Ex:
    $4 + 6 - 2 = 5 + 3$
    $8 = 8$

* <u>Note</u> – numbers are different on both sides of the equal sign, but each side has the same value.

When equations have like variable, you need to get variable on one side and the numbers on the other side of the equal sign (=) to figure out what the value of the variable is. Then substitute the value of the variable for each place the variable appears in the original equation to see if indeed the equation is equal.

* <u>Note</u> – whatever you do to one side of the equal sign, you <u>MUST</u> do the <u>SAME</u> to the other side of the equal sign.

Ex:

    □ + □ + 2 = 8 + □

    □̷ + □ + 2 = 8 + □̷   Remove <u>one</u> box from each side

    □ + 2 = 8   Now you have the variable on only side

    □ + 2 = 8 - 2   Now take 2 away from each side
      - 2

    □ = 6   Now you have the value of the variable

Now replace 6 for all of the boxes in the original equation. Work it out.

Ex:
$$(6 + 6) + 2 = 8 + 6$$
$$12 + 2 = 8 + 6$$
$$14 \neq 14$$

Is each side now equal to each other? Yes
This is your check (proof) that □ = 6

Ex:
$$x + x + x + x + 2 = x + x + x + 9$$
(with arrows pointing to each of the first three x's on each side)

First remove 3 x's from <u>BOTH</u> sides

$$x + 2 - 2 = 9 - 2$$
$$x = 7$$

Now subtract 2 from <u>BOTH</u> sides

$$x = 7$$

$$x + x + x + x + 2 = x + x + x + 9$$
$$(7 + 7 + 7 + 7) + 2 = (7 + 7 + 7) + 9$$
$$28 + 2 = 21 + 9$$
$$30 \neq 30 \qquad \underline{check}$$

Ex:

$x + 3 + 2x = x + 5$ (arrows over the x's on each side)
$ 3 + 24 = 5$
$ 2x = 2$

$$\frac{2x}{2} = \frac{2}{2}$$
$$x = 1$$

Subtract 3 from <u>BOTH</u> sides

Substitute 1 for each x

$x + 3 + 2x = x + 5$
$1 + 3 + 1+1 = 1 + 5$
$ 6 \neq 6 \qquad$ <u>check</u>

Ex:

$2x + (x - x) + 1 = x + 9$ (arrows over the two x's in parentheses)
$ 2x + 1 = x + 9$
$ \cancel{x} + x + 1 = \cancel{x} + 9 \qquad$ Remove one x from each side
$ x + 1 - 1 = 9 - 1$

$ x = 8$

Substitute 8 for each x in the original equation

$2x + x - x + 1 = x + 9$
$(8 + 8) + (8 - 8) + 1 = 8 + 9$
$16 + 0 + 1 = 17$
$ 17 \neq 17 \qquad$ <u>check</u>

Ex:

$2(x + 4) + x = x + 16$
$2(x + 4)$ means $x + x + 8$

$x + x + 8 + x = x + 16$
$x + x + 8 - 8 = 16 - 8$ Remove 8 from each side
$x + x = 8$
$x = 4$

Substitute 4 for each x

$2(x + 4) + x = x + 16$
$x + x + 8 + x = x + 16$
$4 + 4 + 8 + 4 = 4 + 16$
$\quad\quad\quad 20 \neq 20$ <u>check</u>

Roman Numerals

Roman numerals were made over 2,000 years ago, using seven letters to represent numbers. Combining these letters represent larger numbers.

Basic Letters:

Letter		Number
I	=	1
V	=	5
X	=	10
L	=	50
C	=	100
D	=	500
M	=	1000

1 = I		40 = XL (ten less than fifty)
2 = II		45 = XLV
3 = III		50 = L
4 = IV	(one less than five)	55 = LV
5 = V		60 = LX
6 = VI	(one more than five)	65 = LXV
7 = VII		70 = LXX
8 = VIII		75 = LXXV
9 = IX	(one less than ten)	80 = LXXX
10 = X		90 = XC (ten less than 100)
11 = XI	(one more than ten)	95 = XCV
12 = XII		100 = C
13 = XIII		125 = CXXV
14 = XIV	(ten plus four)	150 = CL
15 = XV		175 = CLXXV
16 = XVI		200 = CC
17 = XVII		400 = CD
18 = XVIII		450 = CDL
19 = XIX	(ten plus nine)	500 = D
20 = XX		600 = DC
25 = XXV		900 = CM
30 = XXX		1000 = M
35 = XXXV		2009 = MMIX

Glossary

Absolute Values – The absolute value of a <u>positive</u> number or 0 is that number itself. The absolute value of a <u>negative</u> number is its opposite.

Acute Angle – angles that measure <u>less</u> than 90°.

Acute Triangle – a triangle with <u>all</u> angles <u>less</u> than 90°.

Addend – the parts of an addition problem that are added together.
Ex: In 24 + 32 = 56, 24 and 32 are addends.

Addition – an operation in computation where numbers are put together. Plus sign (+) is used. Ex: 24 + 32 = 56.

Addition sentence – all addends followed by an equal sign and the sum.
Ex: 12 + 6 + 8 = 26.

Adjacent Sides – two sides of a polygon with a common vertex.

Algebra – a branch of mathematics that uses letters as well as numbers to show relationships.

Algebraic Expression – any equation with a missing part. Ex: $x + 8 = 12$

Analog Clock – traditional clock showing seconds, minutes, and hours using a large hand and a small hand.

Angle – the shape formed by two rays with the same endpoint that becomes the vertex.

Arc – a curved part on a circle.

Area – the number of square units that cover the surface of a figure.

Arrange – to put in order.

Array – an orderly arrangement of objects or symbols in rows.

Associative Property – the sum or product is the same regardless of the grouping.
Ex: (3 + 5) + 2 = 3 + (5 + 2)   (3 × 10) × 7 = 3 × (10 × 7)

Average – the mean of a group of numbers found by adding up all numbers then dividing by the amount of numbers added.

Axes – in graphs (grids) the horizontal number line is the x-axis line and the vertical number line is the y-axis line.

Base of a Solid – either the congruent ends or top and/or the bottom of a solid geometric figure.

Base Ten System – our number system based on tens, hundreds, thousands, etc.

Bar Graph – a graph using either horizontal or vertical bars to show information.

Capacity – the amount of units that an object can hold, measured in cubic units.

Cardinal Number – numeration beginning with 1 and 1st, 2nd, etc.

Celsius – a measurement of temperature in the Metric System using units called degrees Celsius, freezing point at 0^0C and boiling point at 100^0C.

Centimeter (cm) – a metric measurement of length equal to $\frac{1}{100}$ of a meter. There are 2.54 centimeters in an inch.

Chord – a straight line joining two points on a circle, may or may not be a diameter.

Circle – a curved-closed figure, with <u>all</u> points on the curve, equal distance from the center point.

Circumference – the distance around a circle found by multiplying the diameter by pi (π) (3.14).

Common Factors – like factors in two or more numbers.

Common Multiples – like multiples for two or more numbers.

Commutative Property – the sum or product is the same regardless of the order of the addends or factors.

Ex: 4 + 2 + 3 = 3 + 4 + 2   3 × 6 = 6 × 3
         9 = 9   18 = 18

Compatible Numbers – when a problem seems overwhelming with extra large numbers, you can simplify it with small numbers to better understand the problem. Estimated numbers are also examples of compatible numbers.

Composite Numbers – numbers that have <u>more</u> than two factors. Ex: 6 = 1, 2, 3, 6

Cone – a space figure having one circular flat surface and one vertex.

Congruent figures – shapes that have identical shapes and sizes.

Coordinates – ordered pairs for plotting points on a grid or graph.

Cubic measurements – the amount of cubes that can fit inside a geometric solid.

Cup (c) - a measurement of capacity equal to 8 ounces of liquid or dry ingredients.

Curve – any line that is not straight, the outer edge of a circle.

Cylinder – a space figure with a curved surface and two parallel bases that are identical circles.

Day – one of 365 units of a year, 24 hours.

Decagon – a polygon with ten sides. A regular decagon has ten equal sides and angles.

Decimal Number – any number less than one whole separated by a decimal point as in money. Ex: $2.75 equals two whole dollars and part of a dollar, 75 cents. The decimal side is on the right of the decimal point.

Degree – unit used in measurement of temperature, angles and parts of a circle. A complete circle has 360 degrees (360°). It is written as a small zero after the number at the top.

Denominator – the number below the fraction line in the fraction. It tells how many total parts are in one whole.

Diagonal – a line segment that joins two non-adjacent vertices of a polygon.

Diameter – a line segment that passes through the center point of a circle and both endpoints are on the circle.

Digit – any single number 0 – 9.

Dimensions – the number of coordinates used to express a position.

Distributive Property – allows you to breakdown numbers and do more than one operation. Ex: 4 × 56 = 4 × (50 + 6) = (4 × 50) + (4 × 6)

Dividend – the number that is divided by another number (the division) in a division problem.

Divisibility – the ability to be divided equally.

Division – the operation of putting a number into equal parts of smaller numbers. Division sign is used (÷).

Divisor – the number by which another number (the dividend) is divided by in a division problem.

Edge – a line segment where two faces of a three-dimensional figure meet.

Endpoint – the point(s) at the end of a ray or line segment.

Equal – when two sides of an equal sign have the same values.

Equilateral Triangle – a triangle with three equal sides and angles.

Equally likely – when the odds of both sides having an equal chance.

Equation – a statement that two sides (quantities) are equal, an arithmetic sentence.

Equivalent – equal in value, amount.

Estimate – to give an approximation rather than the exact answer.

Even numbers – all numbers divisible by 2.

Expanded Form – when a number is put into its basic ten components.
Ex: 3467 = 3000 + 400 + 60 + 7

Exponent – in 10^3, the small 3 is the exponent. It tells how many times the 10 is multiplied by itself.

Ex: 10^3 = 10 × 10 × 10 = 1000. 10^3 is read as ten to the third power.

Expression –any math statement or equation.

Fact Family (related sentence) – are sets of four arithmetic sentences that all have the same numbers, but two opposite operation signs.
Ex: 3 + 7 = 10   6 × 4 = 24
     7 + 3 = 10   4 × 6 = 24
     10 – 3 = 7   24 ÷ 6 = 4
     10 – 7 = 3   24 ÷ 4 = 6

Face – a plane figure that serves as a side of a solid figure.

Factors – are the numbers that are multiplied to get a product.
Ex: 3 × 4 = 12   The 3 and the 4 are the factors.

Fahrenheit – a measurement of temperature using units called degrees. Fahrenheit freezing point is 32°F, and the boiling point is 212°F.

Foot (ft) – a unit of linear measurement in the U.S. Customary Standard Measurement System. Ex: 12 inches = 1 foot.

Figure – geometric shape.

Flip – also called reflection, a transformation of a geometric figure that results in a mirror image of the original.

Formula – a process of operation or set of rules to calculate a problem.
Ex: $A = L \times W$ (area = length times width)

Fraction – a number that represents parts of a whole, written as a number above a number. Ex: $\frac{2}{3}$ = ■■☐ 2 out of 3 parts.

Front-end-estimation – estimating a group of numbers using only the numbers on the far left. Ex: 246 + 892 + 693 = 200 + 800 + 600 = 1600

Gallon (gal) – a unit of measurement used for the capacity of liquid. It is the largest unit of measurement in the U.S. Customary Standard Measurement System for liquids.

Geometry – the branch of mathematics that has to do with points, lines, and shapes.

Gram (g) – a metric measurement of weight. Ex: 1000 grams = 1 kilogram

Graph – a drawing that shows information about changes in numbers.

Greater than – using the symbol > to show that the first number is larger than the second number. Ex: 42 > 17

Greatest Common Factor (GCF) – after listing all of the factors of 2 or more numbers, you find the largest factor that appears in all the groups.

Ex: 8 = 1, 2, 4, 8   12 = 1, 2, 3, 4, 6, 12   GCF = 4

Grid – a network of horizontal and vertical lines that intersect to form squares or rectangles.

Height – the tallness of a geometric figure.

Heptagon – a polygon with seven sides and angles.

Hexagon – a polygon with six sides and angles.

Hexagonal prism – a geometric solid with two bases and seven sides.

Horizontal – a straight line going from left to right.

Hour – one of 24 units in a day. Hours are split in half between AM (midnight to noon), and PM (noon to midnight).

Hundreds – all of the numbers within 100, 200, 300, etc. Ex: 10 × 10 = 100

Hundredths – on the decimal side, the second place on the right of the decimal point. Ex: The amount of ones in one whole such as 9 cents = $0.09 = 9 hundredths of one dollar.

Hypotenuse – the side opposite the right angle of a right triangle, the longest side of a right triangle.

Identity Property – in multiplication, any number times 1 equals the number. In division, any number divided by 1 equals the number. Ex: 3 × 1 = 3, 8 ÷ 1 = 8

Improper fraction – a fraction in which the numerator is greater than the denominator.

Inch (in) – the smallest unit in U.S. Customary Standard linear length measurement. Ex: 12 inches = 1 foot

Inequality – two numbers or figures that are not equal.

Integers – any positive or negative number beginning with zero. Positive and negative numbers are opposite of each other.

Intersect – when one line crosses another, or in two or more sets of numbers, the numbers that are the same intersect the group.

Irregular Polygon – polygons that have unequal sides.

Isosceles Triangle – a triangle that has <u>two</u> congruent sides and angles.

Kilogram (kg) – a metric measurement of weight that is equal to 1000 grams.
Ex: 1 kg = about 2.2 pounds.

Least Common Denominator (LCD) – the smallest common multiple of the denominators in a given set of fractions.

Least Common Multiple (LCM) – the smallest number, other than 0, which is a multiple of each number in a given set of numbers.
Ex: 3 = 3, ⑥, 9, 12, 15, ⑱ .....   6 = ⑥, 12, ⑱, 24, ...   LCM = 6

Left – opposite of right, direction shown by arrow ⬅——— , also refers to a remainder in division.

Length – the measurement of a line or object from end to end, the longer measurement compared to width. Area is length time's width.

Ex: $A = L \times W$
       $A = 12 \times 5$
       $A = 60$ square units

Less than – using the symbol <, shows that the first number is smaller than the second number. Ex: 23 < 48

Line – a collection of points on a straight path that goes on and on in opposite directions. Symbol for a line is ⬅———➡ .

Line of Symmetry – a line dividing a two-dimensional figure into two or more mirror images of each other.

Line Graph – a graph that shows changes in information over time. Points are plotted and connected by lines to show increases and decreases over time.

Line Plots – a vertical graph using X's to show amount for information.

Line Segment – a part of a line with an endpoint at each end. Ex: •———•

Liter (L) – a metric measurement of capacity equal to about one quart. A liter is a little larger.

Lowest terms – the smallest equivalent fraction that can be made by dividing the greatest common factor (GCF) into BOTH the numerator and the denominator.

Ex: $\dfrac{4}{10} = \dfrac{2}{5}$ ÷ by 2

Mass – the quantity of matter.

Mean – same as average.

Measurement – the method of finding the size, weight, dimensions, distance, volume, etc, using the U.S. Customary Standard or Metric System.

Median – the middle number in a group of numbers found by counting how many numbers there are and divide by 2 or keep crossing out extreme end until you have the center number left. Ex: 3̶ 7̶ ⑨ 1̶3̶ 1̶4̶

Meter (m) – a metric measurement of length equal to 100 centimeters or 1000 millimeters or 39.37 inches.

Mile (mi) – a U.S. Customary Standard measurement of distance equal to 5280 feet or 1760 yards.

Milliliter (ml) – a metric measurement of capacity. Ex: 1000 ml = 1 liter

Millimeter (mm) – a metric measurement of length equal to $\dfrac{1}{1000}$ of a meter.
Ex: 10 millimeters = 1 centimeter

Minus – the minus sign (-) is used to show subtraction.

Minute – unit of time equal to 60 seconds, one sixtieth of an hour.

Mixed Number – a combination of a whole number and a fraction. Ex: $2\dfrac{3}{4}$

Multiple – the product of a specific number and any other number.
Ex: Multiples of 4 = 4, 8, 12, 16, 20,..... There is <u>NO</u> end to multiples.

Multiplication – the operation of quick addition of a number, a certain number of times. The times sign is used (×).

Natural Numbers – counting numbers beginning with 1, also called Cardinal Numbers.

Negative Numbers – numbers below zero on a number line, opposite of positive numbers.

Net – a geometric solid that has been opened up so all sides are flattened, but all attached, and can be refolded into the solid shape again.

Numbers – numerals that represent quantity.

Numeral – figure that stands for a number: 1, 2, 3, …

Number sentence – numbers with operation indicator and equal sign.

Ex: 42 + 9 = 51   25 – 5 = 20
      3 × 9 = 27   56 ÷ 8 = 7

Numerator – top number in a fraction, tells the part of the whole.

Obtuse Angle – any angle that measures MORE than 90°.

Octagon – a geometric shape with eight sides and angles. Ex: stop sign

Odd Numbers – all numbers NOT divisible by 2.

Ones – 0 -9, first place position in place value of whole numbers.

Operations – mathematical processes: addition, subtraction, multiplication, and division.

Ordered Pair – a pair of numbers in which the numbers occur in a special order such as coordinates on a map.

Ordinal Numbers – any number such as first, second, third, etc… that shows position in a sequence, 1, 2, 3, 4, …

Ounce (oz) – a measurement of weight. Ex: 16 ounces = 1 pound

Outcome – results in probability problems.

Parallel lines – lines that NEVER intersect.

Parallelogram – a geometric figure that has parallel opposite sides.

Pentagon – a geometric shape with five sides.

Pentomino – a figure made of 5 congruent squares joined edge to edge – must share sides.
Ex:

Perimeter – the distance around a figure.

Perpendicular – intersecting lines that form 90° angles.

Pi (π) – the ratio of the circumference of a circle to its diameter. Pi equals a little more than 3.14.

Pictograph – a bar graph that uses pictures or symbols to represent numbers.
Ex: = 4 books

Pie Graph (circle graph) – a circle divided into sections that show fractions or percents of information.

Pint (pt) – a measurement of U.S. customary standards of capacity equal to 2 cups.

Place value – the value of a digit as representing ones, tens, hundreds, thousands, etc., according to its position or place in a number.

Plane – a flat surface extending infinitely in all directions such as the flat surface of this sheet of paper.

Point – the smallest geometric unit. A position in space, often represented by a dot. (•)

Polygon – a simple, closed plane figure bounded by straight lines.

Polyhedron – a geometric solid bounded by flat faces.

Positive Numbers – all numbers above zero.

Pound (lb) – a U.S. customary standard measurement of weight equal to 16 ounces.

Power – denotes how many times a number is multiplied by itself using an exponent.
Ex: 10^6 is read as ten to the sixth power, which means 10 × 10 × 10 × 10 × 10 × 10 = 1,000,000.

Prime Number – a positive number that has <u>only two</u> factors, the number and one.
Ex: 5 = 1, 5   23 = 1, 23

Prism – a geometric solid with two identical, parallel bases.

Probability – the ratio of favorable outcomes to possible outcomes in an experiment.

Product – the quantity that results from multiplying two or more numbers.

Proper fractions – a fraction that has a smaller number in the numerator than the denominator. Ex: $\frac{3}{7}$

Pyramid – a geometric solid whose base is a polygon and whose faces are triangles with a common vertex, the point where two rays meet.

Quadrilateral – any polygon with four sides.

Quart (qt) – a U.S. customary standard measurement of capacity equal to 4 cups or 2 pints.

Quarter – a unit of U.S. money equal to 25 cents ($0.25) or $\frac{1}{4}$ of a dollar, one fourth of a hundred.

Quotient – the answer found when you divide.

Range – the difference between the least and the greatest numbers in a group of numbers.

Ratio – a comparison of two quantities.

Ray – a part of a line with only one endpoint and goes on and on in only one direction.

Ex: •———▶

Reciprocal – the inverse of a fraction in division of fractions.

Ex: $4 \div \frac{1}{4} = 4 \times \frac{4}{1} = 16$

Rectangle – a geometric figure with four 90° angles and opposite congruent parallel lines.

Rectangular Prism – a geometric solid with six sides (faces), all of which are rectangles.

Rectangular Pyramid – a pyramid with a rectangular base.

Reflection – a flip, to turn a figure over producing a mirror image.

Regroup – often called borrow, to change place value in subtraction.

Ex: 62 = 50 + 12
      -38 = -30 + 8

Regular polygons – polygons that have all equal sides.

Related Facts – facts with the same numbers.

Ex: 7 + 4 = 11   4 × 5 = 20
       4 + 7 = 11   5 × 4 = 20
       11 – 7 = 4   20 ÷ 5 = 4
       11 – 4 = 7   20 ÷ 4 = 5

Remainder – the number that is left over after dividing when it's not even.

Ex: 7 ÷ 2 = 3 R 1   (One is left over)

Rhombus – a parallelogram with equal sides.

Right Angle – an angle that is one-fourth of a circle. A right angle equals 90°.

Right Triangle – a triangle that has one right angle.

Rotation – to *turn* or rotate a figure.

Ex:

Rounding – estimating to the nearest ten, hundred, thousand, etc...

Ex: 23 = 20   482 = 500   8649 = 9000

Scale – how numbers progress in a graph, counting simply by two's, five's, ten's, etc.

Scalene Triangle – a triangle with all three sides that are different sizes.

Second – $\frac{1}{60}$ of a minute, the smallest unit of an hour. In a sequence, after the first is the second, then third, etc.

Semicircle – one half of a circle.

Sequence – placing objects or numbers in order.

Similar – figures that have the same shape but may be different sizes.

Skip Counting – counting in a pattern, by 2's, 10's, etc. The same amount of numbers is skipped in the progression.

Ex: 2, 4, 6, 8, 10, ...

Slide – translation, when a figure moves from one position to another going in the same distance and direction.

Ex:

Solid figure – a closed, three-dimensional figure.

Sphere – a three-dimensional figure formed by a set of points that are all the same distance from a fixed point called the center, a ball.

Square unit – a unit of measure that has a length of one unit and a width of one unit used to measure area.

Statistics – a branch of mathematics in which groups of numbers are compared. It includes collecting, organizing, and interpreting data. Graphs are often used to show this data.

Straight line – no curve, 180°, diameter of a circle.

Subtraction – the operation of "taking away" one number from another number. Minus sign (-) is used.

Sum – the answer in addition.

Surface – part or all of the boundary of a solid. A surface may be flat or curved.

Symmetry – when two congruent shapes are made by folding a figure in half. A dividing line is a line of symmetry.

Table – orderly arrangement of facts and figures.

Tally – marks to record amounts.

Temperature – amount of heat or cold measured by a thermometer.

Tens – second place position on the whole number place value system.

Ex: 2,3<u>8</u>1   8 is in the tens place

Thermometer – instrument used to measure temperature in Fahrenheit or Celsius.

Three-dimensional – relating to objects that have length, width, and depth. Solid geometric figures.

Title – name given to a graph pertaining to the kind of information involved.

Ton – a unit of U.S. customary standard weight equal to 2000 pounds.

Total – the complete sum or product, answer in addition or multiplication, to add up.

Translation – slide, when a figure moves from one place to another without turning or flipping.

Trapezoid – a quadrilateral with only one pair of parallel lines.

Tree diagram – in probabilities, a tree diagram can be used to show all of the possibilities.

Triangle – the smallest of closed figures, three sides and angles.

Triangular Prism – a prism in which the bases are triangles.

Triangular Pyramid – a pyramid with a triangular base.

Turn – a rotation of a figure.

Ex:

Two-dimensional – relating to figures that have length and width but no depth, figures that are flat like a sheet of paper.

Unit – selected amount used in measuring, one of anything.

Unlike fractions – when adding or subtracting fractions that have different denominators.

Variable – the unknown in an algebraic expression represented by a figure or letter.

Vertex – a point at which two line segments, lines or rays, meet to form an angle. Vertices are the plural.

Volume – the number of cubic units inside a geometric solid.

Weight – how heavy an object is. Units of weight include ounces, pounds, tons, milligrams, grams, kilograms.

Width – a side of a quadrilateral shorter than the length.

Yard (yd) – a unit of U.S. customary standard measurement equal to 3 feet or 36 inches.

Year – a measurement of time equal to 365 days. A true year is $365\frac{1}{4}$ days. Leap year is 366 days which is every four years.

Zero Property – in addition, the zero property means any number added to zero equals the number. Ex: $4 + 0 = 4$. In multiplication, the zero property means any number multiplied by zero equals zero. Ex: $4 \times 0 = 0$

Edwards Brothers Malloy
Oxnard, CA USA
September 2, 2014